The Heart of a Village

The Heart of
a Village

An intimate history
of Aldbourne

IDA GANDY

ALAN SUTTON

ALAN SUTTON PUBLISHING
PHOENIX MILL · FAR THRUPP · STROUD · GLOUCESTERSHIRE

First published in 1975 by
Moonraker Press, Bradford-on-Avon

This edition published in 1991

British Library Cataloguing in Publication Data

Gandy, Ida
The heart of a village.
1. Wiltshire. Social life, history
I. Title
942.31

ISBN 0 86299 874 3

Cover picture: April in the Meadows by *W.H. Bartlett.*
Photograph: Fine Art Photographic Library Ltd.
(Courtesy of Bourne Gallery.)

Printed and bound in Great Britain by
The Guernsey Press Co. Ltd, Guernsey, Channel Islands.

Contents

AUTHOR'S NOTE

This book makes no pretensions to being a definitive village history. For that more scholarship and opportunity for deeper research than I can provide are necessary. Rather, it is an attempt to present the picture of a village, set in an isolated position among the Wiltshire downs, that has developed and maintained through a long period of time a sturdy independence and a strong life of its own; a village that has survived hard times and prospered again; which has seen the death of one industry succeeded by the birth of another; which, in spite of many changes, has kept some of its old families for at least 350 years.

I want to acknowledge the deep debt I owe to the late Major Inkpen and his collaborator M. Dibden for the remarkable collection of papers dealing with Aldbourne history which they left behind. Grateful acknowledgements are also due to Richard Sandell; to E. G. H. Kempson, to J. V. Spalding, and to many village friends without whose help this book could never have been written.

I.G.

Foreword

O N an October day in 1826 a broad-bodied man—'just the weight of a four-bushel sack' as he puts it himself, with 'a good sensible face, rather full . . . a ruddy complexion', in a scarlet, broadcloth waistcoat, came riding southwards over the downs from Swindon.

William Cobbett was in high spirits. The previous night he had stayed with a friend and seen 'what I never saw before, four score oxen grazing upon one farm—nearly all fat . . . I should suppose that they were worth, or shortly will be, twenty pounds'. His pleasure is dimmed, it is true, by the thought that they are probably destined for that loathed 'Wen', London, but even so his delight in all he sees that morning conquers. There is Swindon itself 'that very neat, and plain, and solid and respectable market town', and after Swindon the downs, which he loved so much that, 'if I had to choose I would live ever here, and specially I would farm here rather than . . . in the Vale of Evesham or in what Kentish men call "their Garden of Eden" '.

Cobbett's only grievance is that this country seems a little bare. He drops down to the village of Aldbourne—and here he finds himself among trees again. His sharp little grey eyes note the unusually fine Church raised high above the Green; also the houses that encircle it, many no doubt in poor condition. The inhabitants may well have looked dispirited. Pessimism returns.

'This is a town', he declares, 'and was, manifestly, once a large town. Its church is as big as three of that in Kensington' (his home at the time). 'It has a market now, I believe; but I suppose it is, like many others, become merely nominal, the produce being nearly all carried to Hungerford in order to be forwarded to the Jew-devils and the tax-eaters, and the monopolisers in the Wen, and in smaller Wens on the way. It is a decaying place, and I daresay it would be nearly depopulated in twenty years' time, if this hellish jobbing system were to last so long.'

His judgment for that special time was no doubt true. Aldbourne might not have wholly recovered from two devastating fires; many houses were probably not yet rebuilt. And another sad thing had happened less than a year before. The Bell Foundry, which had sent out bells far and wide for 130 years, had recently moved to Whitechapel. James Wells, the bell-founder, was bankrupt. No longer did furnaces blaze behind the church and downs and in the village; no longer did the clang of hammer and anvil ring across the Green. Furthermore a second industry was in slow decline. The Fustian trade which had kept scores of men and women busy since the last quarter of the seventeenth century was slowly dying under the relentless pressure of the Industrial Revolution.

Again, many small men were still feeling saddened or embittered by the loss of their own bits of cornland, their own pastures for a cow or a few sheep, since Parliament passed the Aldbourne Enclosure Act in 1809. But, though right about the decay at that particular time, could Cobbett have cast his hawk-like glance over the village some 120 years later he would have been astonished to see how flourishing, how prosperous, it had grown.

He rides on with his companion past the village pond (no time to learn the famous dabchick tale) past the Fustian factory and the Malthouse; beside the winter-bourne, probably dry at that season, and so to Ramsbury where they stop to bait their horses. Here again he makes one of his scathing judgments. 'This is a large and apparently miserable village,' he writes in his diary that evening.

This verdict on their age-long rival would perhaps have pleased the people of Aldbourne—surely better 'decaying' than 'miserable'. And the epithets Cobbett applies to other Wiltshire places would further have mollified them. Calne is 'a villainous hole'; Wootton Bassett 'a mean, vile place'; Cricklade 'a rascally-looking hole'.

We leave this rumbustious, provocative man to ride up the steep hill to Froxfield and so to Burghclere, and return ourselves to this village which he so mistakenly believed would hardly exist in 20 years time. Mistakenly, because he looked at Aldbourne as an outsider, a mere passer-by, even if a keen-eyed one. He noted dilapidated houses and shabby, sad-looking people. But one important thing was hidden from him; that this place had a heart. A heart that like some human hearts may beat feebly at times but always regain their old vitality.

He noted naturally that it possessed a visible heart in the shape of a Green. But not all villages, even those with Greens, beat strongly again after calamity or frustration. I can think now of one such which looks perfect as you enter it. The Green is shaded by beautiful trees, and round it stand perfect little thatched, whitewashed cottages. The gardens are all terribly trim, weedless, well-cared for. But gradually you realise that something has gone wrong here. Where are the women gossiping at their doors? Where the tangle of flowers, so close that they seem almost talking together? Where are the trees? In the end you would welcome the sight of just one discarded cream carton laying on the grass. All day reigns a strange unnatural silence, broken only by an incoming or outgoing car. The only children you see are correctly dressed little girls riding by on well-groomed ponies.

It is a village—and it is not the only one—which has been taken over by week-enders, or by others who return only to sleep at night and amuse themselves at the weekend. Other villages have grown glossy with smart little over-painted houses, rockeries, garages. Others again have suffered slow decay till they are melancholy ghosts of what they were once.

I hope to show that this village has not only a central, visible heart, where children shout and play round the old Market Cross, where people of all kinds meet and chat, but has also, in spite of the inevitable and quite welcome influx of newcomers, kept its old village aristocracy; the families whose names occur month after month, year after year, in the Parish Registers, some for over 300 years. And further, looking more deeply into reasons for the strength of its heart-beat, it has gained courage and independence in the past from its isolation among the downs, and still draws inspiration, even if often unconsciously, from these hills that enfold it on three sides.

'I will look up to the hills whence cometh my help', is as true to many people today as it was 3,000 years ago.

A NOTE ON ALDBOURNE'S EARLY HISTORY

Aldbourne has had perhaps as rich a history as any village in Wiltshire. People of the Stone, the Bronze and the Iron Ages roamed its uplands; the Romans, as will be seen in 'Beating the Bounds', left ample evidence of their occupation and also of increasing movement from the bare, waterless downs to lower, more fertile country; a movement continued by the more civilised English after their departure.

A period of comparative peace succeeded the stormy years following the Danish invasion, and by the time of Domesday Aldbourne was a flourishing settlement with a well-endowed church. Before the Norman Conquest, the village formed part of the large estates of Ghida, niece of Canute and mother-in-law of Edward the Confessor. But her lands were seized when she refused to recognise William, and the Crown kept its hold till in 1229 Henry III gave the Manor to William Longsword, fourth Earl of Salisbury. Some 100 years later, through a complicated series of marriages, the House of Lancaster took possession and retained it till Charles I sold it to the City of London to pay his debts.

ONE

In and around the Village

TO get a clear idea of the village today we will 'beat the bounds' in the manner of countless Rogationtide perambulations, following not only in the footsteps of old inhabitants but also in those of sturdy bands of walkers today. A retired sailor revived the practice in 1964 when he set off alone to walk the 18½ wayward miles; over fields and by field-paths; over downland; through woods and copses and hedges, and along a short occasional stretch of road. The year after two others joined him; three years later 14, till by 1973 the number rose to over 50, including a man of 78, and several very young children (one child of five achieved 14 miles of the course).

This indomitable band meet at the old Market Cross on the Green to start exactly as the church clock strikes eight. They go southwards from the village, but shortly turn left over a fence, to climb rough steep fields close to a wood called Peg's Hole. Their course now keeps them parallel with the road to Baydon, and brings them past a small clump of trees known as Dor's Grave. Hidden somewhere in the undergrowth is a small tombstone. Like most villages Aldbourne has its time-honoured ghost; and this one is named Dor. His memory survives in a story told by the Vicar of Baydon some 80 years ago. He, 'six feet tall, with nerves of steel' (according to his own account), when walking home at night saw ahead of him a man in a snow-white shirt standing motionless beside the tree clump. 'Another step and I was beside it. Great heavens, it had no head!'. In spite of this disability he resolves to address what he is sure now must be the ghost of Dor, who, so, rumour said, hanged himself at that very spot.

'Unhappy spirit, tell me, God's priest, can I help you?' Not surprisingly, as with the poor little oysters in *Alice in Wonderland*, answer came there none: 'It passed into vapour, leaving no moonlight shadow.'

'And now,' he asked of his readers in *The Marlborough Times*, 'ye scientists, ye religious teachers, what think ye?' No doubt the village postman delivered an extra weight of letters at the Vicarage for many days to come. No other sensational apparition has appeared as far as I know in Aldbourne, though, if the old Romans ever left their graves there would be many.

Leaving Dor's Grave behind they keep along the hedge to the right of the road and cross it at Whitepond Farm. Below lies a little valley formerly called Bankslade Bottom, where once grew an abundance of that charming plant, Salad Burnet (*Peterium sangusorba*). Here a few women came every summer to fill their baskets with the hairy red heads which, so they vowed, made a most delectable wine. But now that sheep no longer graze there and the grass has grown rank and unprofitable you would be hard put to it to find a handful. It seems indeed unlikely that anyone will ever make Burnet Wine again in Aldbourne.

The path now passes above a lonely farm, East Leaze, and brings the boundary-beaters up to Ermine Street, the great Roman road that connected Silchester and Cirencester. Next they mount to Peaks Hill with its crown of beeches, formerly known as Pikewood (meaning a wood with many corners). Here, in 1583, stood a solitary house where lived Thomas Peke, who must have taken his name from the place, rather than the other way round. Till a year ago the silence was broken only by the sound of the wind in the trees, the coo of pigeons, the song of larks, the sharp cry of a kestrel, or, less pleasingly, of a few passing cars. But since the M4 cut its way through the downland (100 yds away to the east) the roar of continuous traffic rends the air. As you stand listening it seems as if every motorist values his time at £1000 a minute.

But walk a little westwards and all is quiet again. And still Peaks Down remains a fine open place for galloping racehorses, for flying kites on a windy day, for lying with a book in the grass. You look down and see Aldbourne folded among the hills; you can watch the sunset in unimpeded splendour, and go home reassured in spite of everything, that the world can still be a goodly place to live in; that is, for the lucky ones.

Step across the road from Peakes Wood and the top of White Horse Hill becomes visible, or, nearer at hand, Ashdown Forest and the shining copper cupola of Ashdown House, built by the gallant Earl of Craven, which sheltered people escaping from the Great Plague, while he remained in London himself to help fight it. Just below, tucked in a fold of the downs, stands an old cottage called Hellsbottom (instance of the way the appropriate letter gets altered with time). For generations the inhabitants fetched their water from the farm half a mile away. Not a good place for a lonely soul, but heaven for a lover of solitude.

The boundary now runs off the Roman road and down the hill, whence it pursues a three-mile course beside the ancient Sugar Way, or 'Socera Weg', i.e. 'Robbers' Way'. With the departure of the

Romans, marauding bands roamed at will over these unguarded lands. And it is down here that Roman occupation has been brought most abundantly to life; indeed some historians place the missing station of Duriconium, between Speen and Cirencester, as nearly as possible at this very spot. The lands of North Farm, just the other side of Sheepwalk Plantation (the long wood that borders this southern side of the Sugar Way) yielded over the years a wealth of Roman pottery and coins covering the period AD 139–169, including one of Alexander Severus and two from Constantinople, one of them picturing the Empress Helena.

When the late Thomas Chandler, owner of North Farm, dug the ground to make a croquet lawn he found so much pottery, so many coins, that he asked a noted Wiltshire archaeologist, B. H. Cunnington, to come and look at them. Mr Cunnington found ample evidence of both an ancient British village and an important Roman occupation. The names of two neighbouring fields, Chestercomb and Popplechurch, bear their own witness. Coins of Ethelred and Alfred suggest a subsequent Saxon settlement. And on top of Sugar Hill, the long lines of downs to which the Sugar Way leads, are the noted Four Barrows. From them and from at least another 21 barrows in the parish, have come stone and bronze axes, arrows and spear-heads, brooches, beads, bracelets, pins and a peculiarly Wessex type of small incense cup—known as the Aldbourne cup—characterised by its flaring mouth, incised ornament and pointville patterns, originally with white inlay.

But to return to our boundary line, which crosses the Swindon road a mile from Warren Farm, climbs the downs again, and drops to Shipley Bottom, where sarsen stones mark the boundary. Here it encounters the Roman road from Cirencester to Mildenhall ('Meinall' to local inhabitants) the Roman Cunetio, and then goes for a short distance along the Herepath, or old Saxon military road. Outside the Parish, a mile to the north, rises Liddington Hill huge Iron Age camp, beloved of Richard Jefferies, and especially rich in downland flowers. A triangle of land marks the meeting-place of three parishes, Aldbourne, Chiseldon, and Liddington. At this point the boundary-beaters have climbed to a height of 800 ft and a magnificent view. Now they drop to another Swindon road, a very busy one, where the children must be carefully guarded as they follow it for about 100 yds.

Then this wayward course takes them to its highest point, 850 ft. Even the lustiest walker goes more slowly, and the old ones positively crave for rest. Sandwiches, coffee, chocolate, are brought out, and everyone sits down. But not for long; many miles lie ahead.

Eastwards they go along a track near a spot where the authorities have chosen to build a vast reservoir for the over-thirsty and ever thirstier town of Swindon. From the Kennet a mile or two to the south-east, water up to 1·3 million gallons are drawn to fill it. Tons of pebbles brought from the Chesil Beech roof it over, to act as a filter against impurities and to preserve moisture. Half a mile away the line turns a little north beside a hedge to encompass the ancient village of Snap, of which more will be said. Round it stretches the Chase that fills so impressive a role in Aldbourne history. Nor far away stands the beautiful grey manor-house of Upham, again closely knit with it for over 500 years. Built of flint and freestone in the mid-sixteenth century, it gradually degenerated into a rather ruinous farmhouse, till rescued and largely rebuilt by Miss Hanbury (later Lady Curry).

For the second time the boundary joins the old Herepath, but quickly turns south to skirt Chase Woods, and through fields to Wilder's Copse—at Rogation-tide full of bluebells, primroses, campion, stichwort—and so into Whiteshard Bottom. Now, up it climbs for half a mile along the oldest and most direct way to Marlborough between hedges of hazel, blackthorn, elder, spindle-berry. Then, in unaccountable fashion, it turns off south, leaving a good solid farmhouse, Stock Close, on its right; crosses the modern road to Marlborough, and runs along Hilldrop Lane towards Ramsbury. A crowd of wood-anemones break gallantly through the brambles on the left. To the south you can see Martinsell, splendid climax to the long line of downs above Pewsey Vale. After passing a small rushy pool called Laurel Pool (but fortunately no laurels) where a pair of mallard love to nest, Aldbourne gives in to Ramsbury and the walkers must face a jungle of copses, bright with bluebells, to Pentico (formerly Penticoots). Here once stood a large farmhouse, but slowly it fell into decay and ended as a target for American soldiers in the last World War.

Now the party faces its most precipitous climb up the grass slopes and on through more tangled copse-land till the southernmost point of the parish is reached. This is Brick-kiln Cottage, more truly a small farmhouse, stoutly built of brick and flint. The house itself is in Aldbourne. Once it was known as the Gin House, so one may justi-fiably assume that a still, probably an illicit one in so remote a spot, existed. Now the walkers meet a more formidable labyrinth called Love's Copse, not too well beloved by tired feet. The family of a Walter Lof gave it the name. Here the boundary grows more mischievous than ever, so that a slight argument is liable to take place. Anyway, the party is now set on a downward course to Crowood. Once they leave this behind they are irretrievably com-mitted to the course of the winterbourne. Strictly speaking, and occasionally someone persists in being strict, they must in one place at least wade through the middle of the stream, which may be just a weedy, muddy ditch, or a lively sparkling brook. Apart from the often wet and squelchy ground, and a diabolical hedge to scramble through, their troubles are now over.

Somewhere between four and five o'clock they arrive back at the Green, to stand triumphantly beside the Cross, or drop with deep relief on to the grass. A good 18 miles over rough, up-and-down country is something to remember with pride, and, in spite of the hardships, with pleasure.

BELOW THE CHURCH

Happily, Aldbourne follows no set pattern. It has the charm of fortuitousness, so essential a feature of the true English village. The casual visitor, the passing motorist, may find its layout a trifle baffling, but that does not matter. And at all events the Church stands as a landmark, guarding the village like one of Michael's own angels; in splendid isolation, so far, but with houses clustered close below. The Green stretches in front, and on it stands the Market Cross, its 15-ft column crowned by a small cross set at an angle of about 45 degrees. Probably it has always so lain, for a very beautiful watercolour by Buckler of 1866 (referred to later) shows it in that position. The fact that repairs and replacements have taken place makes absolute certainty difficult.

In 1764 the Court Leet judged the small cross to be dangerous and ordered an exact replica. Five years later the whole structure was out of repair, and William Bacon was presented for 'clandestinely carrying away the ruins' and 'of being so unkind as to lay them on the common highway, to the prejudice of many people'. Some ten years ago the little cross had once more to be replaced, again in the position of its predecessor, considered a unique one. The cross itself is clearly one of those frequently erected in the Middle Ages by the religious orders as stations for preaching and for proclamations by the Manor Court. The Court Rolls from 1732 refer constantly to this cross as meeting-place for the jury, whether to beat the bounds or to inspect the chimneys which, ill-kept, menaced all the houses round.

The Green was once the Market Place, and the Court Leet was much concerned with keeping it clean. In 1762 it indicted Stephen Newth and John Sly (who lived in what is now Pond House) for having a dung-heap there, and ordered them to remove it within a month, while Caleb Pizzie was ordered to take up his saw-pit and 'a parcel of timber'.

The Market once played an important part in village life. The earliest mention, in 1311, runs, 'There is a weekly market on Thursday' (possibly Tuesday) 'which "is worth p.a. 26/8"!' In a survey of the Manor in 1590 we learn that 'a weekly Tuesday market was held in the Town of Alborn till within ten years past and sithence the same is and hath been discontinued for upwards of a century'. This was a temporary stoppage. Increased prosperity clearly revived the market, as the Post Office Directory for 1848 speaks of its 'being discontinued for upwards of a century'.

The pleasant, long white house just opposite the Cross, now the Vicarage*, was almost certainly the Market House. The ceiling of the ground floor is made of heavy oak, and grains of corn cropped up in it during repairs. In 1629 Charles I gave Aldbourne special Market Rights, as being part of his Duchy of Lancaster. 'All the People and Tenants', are 'excempt . . . by virtue of divers Grants and Letter Patent of divers former Kings of England for the exaction of Payment of the above pannages, passage and hastage, Stallage, all . . . Fairs, Markets, Towns . . . whatsoever within and throughout our Kingdom.' An old Aldbourne farmer has sometimes waved a copy of this document (translated from the Latin) in Swindon Market.

Just west of the cross stood the inevitable Stocks, always placed near the Church to give a maximum of publicity, and to remind delinquents how hard is the way of sinners. These stocks are shown in a watercolour of the Church made by Buckler in 1866, now in Devizes Museum. In 1762 the Court presented them being out of repair and ordered the Constable to have them mended within a month, or pay £5. A similar injunction appears in 1769. Eleven years later they are reported in very bad condition, but since no mention occurs again it seems likely they were left to rot; stocks by this time were in far less frequent use, though in some places they continued as late as 1865.

At one time animals: ponies, donkeys, pigs and geese, grazed on the Green, but the coming of the motor-car made them a danger, and now it is a happy playground for the children; a good place, too, for a quiet gossip. The windows of the houses set all round give ample opportunity for a survey of just what is going on. One old lady regularly used a pair of binoculars inside her cottage; outside, she stood on wide flat feet, her corgi behind her, turning her head this way and that to make sure she missed nothing. Further down is Bell Court, a name that tells its own story, for here Robert Wells cast many of his bells. Much remains to be said of them.

This bit of the village is alive with history. The Post Office was once the George Inn, and here the Manor Court met. Next door lived the fustian manufacturer, Edward Witts. The immense thickness of the walls of both houses, and the timbering of the ground-floor ceilings testify to their age. Down the rest of the street are old, red-tiled houses. One, until recently, was a little shop full of a variety of goods, from dog-food and bird-seed to knitting wools and

---

*Sad to say this is no longer so. A new Vicarage has been built on the steep hillside, very close to the church, against the wishes of practically the whole village.

dolls, reminiscent somehow of the shop in *Alice Through the Looking-Glass*, and kept by one of the most skilful needlewomen in all the country round.

Now you pass the pleasant, be-flowered Crown Inn, and the seat where old men sit to sun themselves and exchange sly jokes about the passers-by. Beside the seat is a great sarsen stone, one of many scattered about the village. This one may seem nothing much, just like all the rest, but take another look and you will see a small deep hole. It is in fact a blowing-stone; not as powerful as the famous one in the Vale of the White Horse, but with similar properties. Many years ago boys discovered they could produce a wonderful noise from that small hole; too much indeed for the inhabitants of neighbouring houses, so the blacksmith plugged it with iron. When later this was pulled out the old stone refused to speak again, for the hole had lost its original contours. Opposite you now is a handsome Georgian House, called Pond House, very appropriately, since not only does it stand beside the Pond, but in very wet weather another pond would ooze up through its floor. On one of its windows a member of the Sly family scratched his name.

But here the Pond itself must take precedence of all else.

THE POND

Though what you now see before you is only a poor little concrete, urban affair, this was formerly a large and important piece of water, referred to in old maps and deeds as the Town Pond. Cows regularly drank at it, and the fire-engines drew their water from it; children paddled when it was not too muddy. Then one day a strange bird appeared on the water; a dapper little dark fellow who kept diving and re-appearing. People stared. No one had ever seen the like. 'Whatever be 'e?' they asked one another. They went to the oldest inhabitant, and at his command put him in a wheelbarrow. 'Wheel oi round', he ordered: then 'Wheel oi round agen.' After three turns he pronounced the bird a dabchick. This wheeling round of the oldest inhabitant when some strange object had to be identified crops up in other Wiltshire tales.

For Ramsbury folk all the excitement over a bird they could see any day on the River Kennet became a source of endless ribaldry. They loved to tease Aldbourne by tying a dead dabchick to the back of its carrier's cart, and to taunt individual inhabitants with a cry of 'Dabchick!' They did this once too often when a man driving along in a small cart shouted the hated epithet. A minute later he found himself and his cart in the pond—nor was he the last to be so treated. But as the years went on Aldbourne's attitude to its dabchick changed, and has become a source of pride. Nobody but a true native may claim the title, unless he just allows himself to be ducked in the pond.

An interesting fact is that a dabchick is engraved on a number of small bells, sheep and horse bells, cast by the famous Aldbourne Bell Founders, the Cors. Since they cast their last bell in 1757, the dabchick has clearly been linked with the village for over 200 years.

No other noticeable birds have appeared on the Pond till a year or two ago a pair of mallard, one with a broken wing, took refuge there. Scarcely had they landed when men arrived to drain the water away and paint the floor of the pond sky-blue to brighten it up for the Feast; a surprising decision taken by the Parish Council when it was either in exuberant mood or too exhausted by a long meeting to realise what it was doing. The duck flew away, but the broken-winged drake received a comfortable home at the Crown Inn and lives there still with a new mate.

Most old inhabitants remember their old pond with regret, even though clearly it grew increasingly muddy as the years went on. Unfortunately the springs that fed it could not compare with those that keep Bishopstone pond, over the hill in the White Horse Vale, deep and clear.

ROUND THE VILLAGE

Here, in front of the Pond, is the centre of village life. Old men sit on a seat sheltered from the wind to chat and exchange gossip; young mothers with prams gather; others, intent on quick shopping, chat far longer than they intended. Close round are several shops.

Some 60 years ago the butcher carried on a still busier trade than today. On an outside stall stretched the carcases of young pigs holding oranges in their mouths. Instead of a deep-freeze or a refrigerator, joints hung freely from the ceiling, a fact which a certain old shepherd fully appreciated. Returning tired and hungry with his dog in the evening, he would cast a searching glance at the shop, and should it appear empty of customers, and the butcher busy in the back region, he would whistle softly to his dog and murmur 'Hey, Jim!' In a twinkling Jim would jump over the half-barrier and back again with a leg of mutton in his mouth. When the shepherd reached home in the Butts, there on his doorstep Jim waited with his prize. Many must have known about it but were unwilling to tell. Surely, they would say, the shepherd, spending long, cold hours among his sheep on the down, living but sparsely, has earned his right to an occasional feast of mutton?

Close by stands the Old Bakery, but, alas, no home-made bread is now for sale in the village, and no longer do women bring their loaves to the bakehouse that stood behind the Forge. No longer, happily, does the baker work long hours into the night.

ON ROUND THE VILLAGE

Leaving the Pond on your left and a little island of shops on your right, you cross the Hungerford road for Castle Street, formerly

Calf Street. This change of name shows how mistaken was the idea that it bore any connection with Lewisham Castle, up on the hilltop; a mysterious place of which little is known. A trench, hidden deep in undergrowth, suggests an ancient fortification, and loose building stones a possible medieval castle. A myth that the Dauphin held it during the French Wars remains completely unauthenticated.

On the north side of Castle Street is a fine old house with a massive chimney, and a barn where timber for the chair-making industry was sawn. Climb on up the street and you come eventually to Dudmore Lodge, a central point in Aldbourne Chase, famous in early hunting days and during the Civil War. Turn right at the lower end of the street and you are in the Butts, where once every able-bodied man had to practise archery. But before you enter it, another right-hand turn takes you up to a big Egg-collecting Depot which handles 100,000 eggs a week. Now back to the Butts, which the 1851 Census shows to have been almost exclusively occupied by agricultural labourers, manual workers, and a small shop or two. Now, when old thatched cottages have proved too tempting a bait, it is a very different story.

At the far end of the Butts, in the past ten years, has risen a colony of red-brick houses and bungalows, built on a piece of ground once called 'Garlands', because there lads gathered nosegays for their sweethearts from an unusual wealth of wild flowers; sadly the name has been corrupted to Garlings.

UP THE SOUTHWARD

You are now at the foot of the Southward (always pronounced 'Southard'). Follow the steep hedged lane, beloved of goldcrests, and stand for a long stare at the top: at the village beautifully set among its downs, and at Greenhill, outlined with trees, away to the east. If you take the western road you reach Ewen's Farm, owned by the Wentworth family, one of those small, self-sufficient farms that grow rarer year by year. A severe drought once brought tragedy here, when five children drank from a stagnant pond and died. They lie together in a central part of the churchyard.

Two paths up on top of the Southward lead south to Ramsbury; one by Hilldrop Farm, one by Love's Copse. On the hillside to the left lies a piece of ground of some 50 acres known as 'The Poor's Allotment', or 'Poor Man's Gorse'. The Enclosure Act of 1802 awarded it for the use of the poor of Aldbourne 'for the time being and forever' for the cutting of furze and other fuel. Among the first trustees was Broome Witts, Fustian maker. He and his fellows laid down elaborate conditions for the use of the land. All fuel had to be carried on the back, though later they conceded that, since a number of poor old people could not manage this, someone appointed by a special trustee might carry it for them. No furze or wood might be sold; it must be kept for the sole use 'of the poor person or family bringing it in'. Only the old and poor of the parish had cutting rights. When a thatcher helped himself to some hazel-wood, the trustees talked of prosecuting him, but he was let off with a fine and a promise not to offend again. If anyone grazed his cattle there he was to be prosecuted, and the informant received a reward of 10s.

During the nineteenth century and early in the present one much of the gorse that the old people brought down with them went to heat the bread ovens; a reminder of one of Christ's homely country similies about the grass 'which tomorrow is cast into the fire'. Many who still enjoy the luxury of an open hearth know what rewarding heat dead branches of gorse can provide.

After 20 years a public meeting decided that better use could be made of the land, and that farmers might graze their cows there from 8 May to 31 October on payment of £3–£4 a year. A cow-keeper received a wage of 6s. a week; a boy to help him, who probably did most of the work, only 13s. for 23 weeks. The man's weekly wages rose later to 8s. and the boy's to £1 for the quarter; but when a girl helped she was paid only 1s. 6d. for 13 weeks. Some 12 to 15 farmers started to graze their cattle on this land, Broome Witts among them, and the money so acquired provided coal and wood at Christmas for old people. The expenses included payment for the passage of coal through the turnpike, and to the Crier for making public announcements.

Something was always happening to Poor Man's Gorse to involve earnest discussion among the Trustees. Neighbouring landlords complained of the plague of rabbits that found cover there, and once a fire, probably a deliberate one, devastated the land. Old people still struggled up the hill for fuel, and sometimes received—unlawfully—a compassionate lift home. In springtime the wood-gatherers reaped a double reward when a nightingale sang from a thorn-bush in full daylight; it may still sing if a bush remains for it. It was a pleasant peaceful place, where tired women could sit and look across the valley to Greenhill. But all fuel-gathering ceased in 1950, when the highest bidder secured sole grazing-rights and was allowed to plough up Poor Man's gorse. Distribution of wood and coal continues today, though not without its problems.

Back at the foot of the Southward you turn right and pass along Farm Lane, where stand attractive council houses, built before the economy drive set in. At the Hungerford road turn left and a few yards bring you to a fine barn, formerly a malthouse, topped by a weather-cock in the shape of a maltster, shovel in hand, and who once had a pipe in his mouth. Originally he was made of stout wood, well over 100 years ago, and 80-year-old inhabitants remember him as a familiar figure in their youth, as did their fathers before them. In 1910 he was repaired, still with his pipe. but in 1966 he fell into a bad way; boys had used him as an Aunt Sally, and tried to knock out his pipe. This time iron took the place of wood and his pipe was not restored; perhaps to save him from further attacks.

The Barn itself is of considerable interest. Not only was corn malted in it for a long time, but subsequently it became a theatre. In 1910 an original play was acted there; an event still remembered by many because for the first time all the actors were real village people. More about it will follow. Go on from the Malthouse and you will notice a solid brick building with Gothic windows standing a little back from the road. This was once the old Fustian factory. Now walk, traffic free, along the right-hand bank of the brook, so lively at times, so undeniably squalid when no water flows. And, such is the nature of the chalk soil where the springs rise that its volume depends on the rainfall three years beforehand.

Now, returning to your path by the stream, you leave a good Georgian house on its banks, and pass a row of old red-tiled cottages, one of which houses the Forge. Few horses now come to be shod, but a bright fire lights up the darkness and shines on the lean, keen face of the smith, descendant of one of the oldest village families, and shows him busy repairing machinery, tinkering with pots and pans, or, what he most enjoys, making weathercocks, gates, fire-screens and so on. Turn right and you are in Oxford Street, and at the foot of Baydon Hill. Somewhere here stood the Workhouse which Aldbourne was ordered to build in 1802.

Higher up the hill one of the old houses was formerly a small inn called 'The Sign of the Windmill', why you will soon understand. Its cellars are still there but nobody remembers it, or knows the date of its closure. Opposite, at the junction with Lottage Road stood once a bleak, windowless little Blind House or Lock-up, pulled down some 40 years ago. An old man, not long dead, told how he and other boys would stand on each other's shoulders to peer and mock the occupants through a narrow grating. It was last used when, after a fire near Love's Farm, the farmer treated the firemen so liberally that they found themselves in the Blind House. Early in the morning came their women-folk with a large teapot of beer, and a spout long enough to reach down through the grating to the wide open mouths below. Close to the Blind House was the Pound for straying cattle, often referred to in the Court Books.

A windmill, on the highest point of the hill, was working till around 100 years ago, when modern machinery put it out of action. It stood idle for many years, and when at last in 1900 its owner decided to pull it down it resisted obstinately, dying as hard as possible. The last miller was a very God-fearing man, who would never allow his mill to work on the Sabbath. Always as the church clock struck twelve on Saturday night, no matter how much corn waited to be ground, no matter how merrily the wheel was turning, out he went to stop it. Not till midnight on Sunday would he allow it to work again.

Turn east at the foot of Baydon Hill and you are in Lottage, 'Lutwyk' in 1299. Its population in 1851 consisted largely of agricultural labourers and willow weavers, but the growth of Swindon has brought new houses and newcomers. One colony of them is called Kandahar, because an old soldier who fought there so named his house. Continue eastwards and you reach the source of the winterbourne. When the water-table was higher than now a flood of water poured down a big upland field in the spring, and still in a wet season Lottage suffers most. One sad day a few years ago a little boy was swept down the stream and drowned under one of the bridges. The winterbourne disappears under the ground at Goddard's Lane, so named after the famous Aldbourne family. A right turn at the end of Lottage leads you back to the Green and to the district once always known as Hightown; a title now usually confined to the big house, in the yard of which stood the famous racing stables. And long before, as we shall see later, lived a colony of willow-weavers.

Climb on up past the Blue Boar, oldest of all the existing village pubs, round the skilfully built walls of Crooked Corner, and you reach Court House, headquarters of the Bell Foundry for over 100 years. In 1809, the Enclosure Act allotted it to be the Vicarage, which it remained till 1956. In those earlier days it may have served the parson well, but later it became a bit of a headache. Experts place the oldest part of Court House at around 1482, but the cellars, of immense strength, with partly half-timbered walls, point to a much earlier house, so the tradition that connects it with John of Gaunt may possibly be true. According to the Patent Rolls for the Duchy of Lancaster an order went out in 1406 'for conies for the use of his household in the Towne of Aldebourne'. There is nothing, however, to show that the Manor Court ever met here. We do know that in 1690, when Elizabeth Bond was Lady of the Manor, it functioned as what is now the Post Office. Court House was originally thatched, but in 1850 tiles replaced the thatch.

The Foundry occupied the north-east part of the grounds. The old Pigeon House, referred to in a bell-founder's will, is still there, to testify how important this place once was.

Grazills, a corruption of Grasshills, is the district beyond Court House. Until new houses sprang up, allotments occupied the land. The row of four barrows lies north at the end of a broad grassy track, known as Haydons; once no doubt Haydowns. It is a favourite haunt of birds when hips and haws ripen in its hedges, and a popular exercising place for dogs. From here the church tower can be seen rising beautifully between the trees.

Cut back to the village, down the field west of the church, and you are in Church Lane, beside the well-designed modern school. This lane, sparsely populated now, housed (according to the census) 50 people in 1851, including a dressmaker, a tailor, a woodman, a shepherd, a willow-weaver, as well as the blacksmith's forge and the Post Office. Here, too, stood a small Baptist chapel and graveyard. The chapel, the oldest in the village, was pulled down many years ago. At the end of the lane is West Street, once far more populous. Though all its houses are old, that formerly called 'Cors' after the bell-founders of that name who once occupied it, is the oldest in the village. It dates from the second half of the fifteenth century, and is surely the most beautiful, with its stone walls, gables and red-tiled roof. In the kitchen-garden still stands a small shed, all that remains of a school. An immense thatched barn known as 'Curs', again after the bell-founders, beautifies the yard, but is a source of continuous anxiety to its owner since thatchers are a dying race and thatching a huge expense. To add to his dilemma a cruel wind, rushing down between the hills not long ago, sent a tall elm crashing on to the roof, destroying some of the fine timber work inside. Fifty yards further north is a small, still older barn, dating from the late fifteenth century, named Woodleys.

Last of all the West Street houses is the solid red-brick Manor, home of the last Lords of the Manor till the title lapsed in 1892; but still the home of the man who farms the Manor Farm, with its 930 acres and fine flock of sheep. Another house at the southern end of the street calls for special mention. This is West Street house, adjoining the Mason's Arms, but once the inn itself. Every Friday, as we know from a Trade Directory for 1792, a stage-wagon that left London on the previous Tuesday arrived at its door, probably until well on into the first half of the nineteenth century. A village woman who died in 1930, aged ninety, loved to tell how her father drove the coach. Money for fares was paid through a small hatch in the house next door –at that time part of the inn itself, later a baker's shop and then a greengrocer's. In the big walled garden of West Street House stands a ruined summerhouse, strangely ornamented outside by 11 pairs of skulls, probably sheep skulls, their eye-sockets filled in with small beer bottles.

Opposite West Street House is the Queen Victoria, an inn until 1971, and favourite haunt of older village men. But the owners thought that three other inns were enough to satisfy the needs of Aldbourne and they sold it. Now it houses an attractive Craft Shop. Cross the road, keep the little island of shops on your right, and you are back in front of the Pond.

How can I best put into words the impression that the village as a whole gives me? As I said before it aims at no set pattern, and yet there is a unity in its layout: in the way it spreads itself below the Church; in the solidity of the small red-tiled houses and the chalk-

and-sarsen stone cottages with their kindly thatched roofs to protect them from damp, from heat, from cold; and in the walls in which the village is so rich—stone-topped, tiled or thatched—walls of unusually fine workmanship. So that perhaps the most vivid impression of the older, central part of Aldbourne is that it was built by men with a concern for the future. Perhaps one day we shall be able to afford this again. Enchanting views of the village may be had from many vantage points, but in the end I believe we must come back to the Pond. To stand on its south side, with all the white-washed, red-roofed houses forming a rambling pattern round it and the church towering behind, is to find at last a good word for that little pond—it mirrors the church.

THE CHASE

Above the village to the west stretches the wide rolling upland known as the Chase; once wholly uncultivated, richly wooded, and scene not only of fighting in the Civil War, but of innumerable poachings, attacks and counter-attacks between the villagers and the owners of sporting rights. Within it, too, existed a famous rabbit warren. Records of its ownership, of hunting rights, of rights to take 'conies' and to cut wood, through the fourteenth, fifteenth, sixteenth and seventeenth centuries, make complicated but fascinating reading.

The Manor of Aldbourne and the Chase became royal property after Ghida, mother of Edward the Confessor, niece of Earl Godwin, refused to recognise William the Conqueror. Later Henry III gave it to William Longsword, Earl of Salisbury, the gransdon of Fair Rosamund, in 1229. By a succession of marriages it passed to the Duchy of Lancaster in 1399 and with them remained till Charles I sold it to the City of London. From the early fourteenth century a great many people hunted there, prominent among them the Walrond family, descendents almost certainly from Walderonde, head forester to William the Conqueror at his royal Manor of Aldbourne. In 1306 William Walronde paid 7s. 6d. in the form of a pound of pepper for the hunting rights, which were maintained by seven generations of his successors. In his will of 1610 Roger Walrond refers to these privileges as the 'roundership, custodie and keeper-shype, and wardenship of the Chase Forest and Warren. In 1481 John and Thomas are called on to take reasonable care of the underwood and also of the 'vine hedges' (otherwise hops) growing within their land. In 1307 the Commissioners of Oyer and Terminus 'sued the Persons who broke the park of Henry de Lacy, Earl of Lincoln and his free chases and warrens of Aldeborn, hunted there and carried away deer, hares, rabbits and partidges'.

And so it goes on year after year; perpetual struggles between the inhabitants of Aldbourne, trying to assert the rights they firmly believed to be theirs, and between rival landowners. In 1311 a complaint was made that the profits amounted to nothing on account of the wild beasts infesting the Chase. Polecats and foxes abounded, but could an occasional wolf still have found cover there? Certainly they were still killed sometimes in various parts of England up to 1496. In 1467 John Elmet, Vicar of Aldbourne, complained that whereas William Walrond and two others have enjoyed the rights of Church Lands on the Chase on condition they paid all charges due for the upkeep of the Church, amounting to 25 marks— 6s. 5d. a year, they have in fact paid nothing.

In 1537 Thomas Walrond was accused of 'riotous hunting', and William Burdett, 'Groom of the King's Stable, Woodward of the Chase of Aldbourne', charged the same Thomas, 'always an enemy of woods and coppices, as his father before him, did felde seven acres of wood . . . and sold them to his own behove and profit'. He also cut down two acres 'to make cart bodies'. The case grew in perplexity when Thomas made charges against Thomas York, who possessed limited rights to the conies, but 'dayly cometh with his servantes into the Chase with bows and arrows, and sometimes a priest of the said York, comes with his crossbow to kill the King's dere'. Furthermore this York prevented Walrond from the 'occuppy- enge of a Lodge; . . . called Dudmore Lodge, and did not suffer him to cut derebrowse for the dere, nor fuel expended in his house like others of his ancestors'.

Waldrond also complained that York kept such 'multitude of conies they do louse yerly eleven akers of land', and called a number of old inhabitants to bear witness to his age-long rights to the Lodge. One old man aged 84 said he knew Thomas Walrond's maternal great-grandfather, William Ingram, and that he had been Keeper of the King's game, and 'held his office by horn, and occupied Dudmore Lodge'. He also testified that Thomas Walrond was allowed fuel for his house, and as much hedgewood for his hedges as he needed, he himself had been underkeeper and had occupied a part of Dudmore Lodge. This, York emphatically denied, and supported his case by a command from no less a person than Sir Thomas More, the Lord Chancellor. He declared also that he himself had cut down his conies to 500, and had killed no deer except under orders from Sir Edward Darrell, whose family were Masters of 'The King's Chase of Aldbourne at that time'. These famous conies will come into the story later. We return now to poaching and timber cutting.

In 1559 three Gilbert brothers petitioned the House of Lords for being committed wrongfully to the Fleet for hunting in the Chase, 'where, without their Lordships' assistance they must spend all their lives without hope of liberty'. After more petitions and counter- petitions their rights in the Chase seem to have been recognised, for we find a Gilbert as Master of the Warren as late as 1724. In that same year (1559) the Chase was the scene of a far more serious event, namely the death of a keeper during an encounter with a poaching gang of Aldbourne men who were hunting the conies of Vincent Goddard, their Master, with two nets called 'the hayes'. The keeper was badly wounded and died next day. Two of the poachers were indicted for murder, but were later pardoned after 'the justices of the Assize' ruled that the charge should have been one of homicide. There was a less serious encounter in 1636. A shepherd, snaring a partridge, was accosted by 'a great Fatte gentleman' hawking on Upham Down. The shepherd threw his prong at him 'and mist him verie narrowle', but killed his gun-dog. The fat gentleman was none other than Thomas Goddard whose effigy kneels devoutly (with his family) in Aldbourne Church. Before he galloped away he shouted to the shepherd that he knew him well and that it should be 'a dear partridge for him', as there can be little doubt it was. For Thomas Goddard, late High Sheriff for Wiltshire, was not likely to allow his assailant, whose 'evil demeanour had affronted him', to get off lightly.

In that same year another of the Goddard family was concerned in a Star Chamber action. Goddard the Younger, whose father was a copyholder within the Manor of Ogbourne, invaded an 'enclosure in His Majesty's Chase', where in winter the young deer were carefully tended. Here the Keepers lodged and went in and out with their hounds, while in the spring they released those young deer to roam freely. This young Goddard, under cover of going to kill conies, 'did with his father's orders, and accompanied by two others, go with dogs, kill a young deer and convey it home'. Goddard boiled it, shared it with the servants, and told them it was mutton. But someone revealed the secret, whereupon the servants were committed to the Fleet; the male Goddards were fined £500 each, Mrs Goddard £50, and all bound over for good behaviour in future. It seems probable that only a small portion of these Star Chamber fines were in fact exacted. Usually they were compounded for a small sum, and we may hope the innocent servants were set free.

Coming now to timber-cutting rights, in 1606 the Overseers for the Duchy woods in Southern England, which included Aldbourne Chase, reported 'that the coppices require considerable fencing by new hedges', but added in a memorandum, 'the inhabitants will not suffer certain copses (including Hillwood and Snape Park) to be fenced at any time', claiming their age-long right to both the timber and the conies. The sturdy independence of Aldbourne people is borne out by the way they seem to have carried their point, and the Commissioners reported that 'there will be no woods saleable these eight years' in consequence.

Their sturdy resistance to any filtering away of their rights continued, and increased when the outbreak of the Civil War made life still harder for them. They began to invade the Chase in large bands, in such numbers that the Earl of Pembroke, in 1643, sought 'protection of his Chase of Aldbourn in Wilts from destruction or any spoil or waste by the tumultuous and riotous assembling together of multitudes'. In that same year a far different assembly invaded the Chase, not riotously nor tumultuously, but with grim determination; intent, not on killing conies or cutting timber, but on the slaughter of as many of their fellow countrymen as they could. Instead of crack of axes and cry of small furry creatures, the air resounded with the thunder of horses' hooves and the roar of guns. From the west the Earl of Essex hastened with his Cavalry and a large body of Foot. From Oxford Prince Rupert marched day and night with 5,000 men to stop the enemy's progress to London. More about this fighting will follow.

Meanwhile, down in Aldbourne itself, wooding, and the killing of an occasional deer, grew ever harder. Not only did the Chase never recover fully from the damage caused by the Civil War, but more astringent measures were taken to deprive the villagers of their former wooding rights until, in the Churchwardens' Accounts appears this item; 'On the 6th January 1703 Richard Stewart and Martha Lamborne were, by order of Mr Jones, Justice of the Peace, whipped publicly in Aldbourne for stealin of wood in ye Chase.' But at least good fat rabbits found their way into our pots a long time after that.

In 1794, Thomas Davis, in his survey *Agriculture in the County of Wilts* writes, 'There is on the downs a track of some hundreds of acres of land, called Albourn Chase, which may truly be called "waste land" and is . . . a blot on the country being merely a cow common all the summer, while the sheep, for which a quarter part of it is much better calculated, are starving for want of it.'

Aldbourne today can be proud of its sheep, some of which feed on the Chase, though much of it is now under the plough.

THE WARREN

But, in one respect at least, the Chase was never as celebrated as The Warren in its north-east corner, once populated by a famous breed of rabbits. This fame they owe particularly to John Aubrey, that highly prized Wiltshire writer, who roamed the county in the eighteenth century, and brought an immense zest, humour, power of observation, and faculty for picking up odd scraps of information wherever he went. The Warren rabbits he describes as 'the best, sweetest, and fattest in England . . . a short, thick coney' and, of the Warren itself, 'The grass there is exceeding short and burnt up in hot weather . . . 'tis a saying that conies love roast meat'.

In the next century the Earl of Oxford, on a journey through

Hants, Wilts, and Berks to Oxford, writes to his wife, 'we passed over Aldbourne Chase, a very famous place for rabbits, and fine they were, we bought a couple, and they answered their character well when dressed'. Their reputation stems from very early days. As far back as 1307 the Calendar of Patent Rolls makes special mention of them. Forty years later the profits of the conies between Michaelmas and Lent are valued at 100s.

In 1311 the Black Prince enters the story, when he sends an order to his 'Warren of Aldbourne to take sixty live conies to his bailiwick and deliver them to the Prince's bachelor . . . towards stocking a little place which he has in these parts'. Next it is John of Gaunt who requires them for the use of his household in 'The Towne of Aldbourne'. On 1 November 1405 his Treasurer at Kenilworth Castle orders John Neale and Richard Bosworth 'to take carriage of conies and other necessaries'. In 1425 'The Farm of Conies within the Chase park and Warren of Aldbourne' is granted to John Walrond . . . 'from the Feast of St Michael . . . for ten years. He must bear the burden of upkeep . . . and at the end of his term to let it pass back in the same good state or better as he received it'.

The Walronds continued these rights for longer than ten years, though evidently they passed, or a portion of them at all events, into other hands. For in 1581 a Thomas Walrond complained that 'York's conies have so disturbed Dudmore Copse that it is worth nothing'. To this York retorted 'there hath been no sale of conies for twelve years'. Many others attained special rights over the rabbits, and to show how important these were John Adee issued a trade token in 1656 depicting three. Leaving the numerous disputes about the conies we take a leap forward of some 70 years and nearly 100 since Aubrey wrote.

We come to a fascinating report by a Cambridge professor of Botany, Professor Richard Bradley, in 1724, based on what he learns from Mr W. Gilbert, 'Master of the famous Warren now upon Auborne Chase'. 'Auborne Chase' he writes, 'which hath of long date been allowed to produce the best rabbits in England. The soil is chalk. The surface hardly more than two inches in thickness. I could not find any other herb growing upon it than nettles, ragwort and silver weed. And yet they are very fat even in the dryest summer, even in the most severe winter; their kidneys can hardly be discovered for the fat that is upon them . . . The fodder given to the rabbits in winter, besides the fine hay . . . is chiefly the hazel, whose bark they devour very greedily.' And again, 'They are admired for the extraordinary sweetness of their flesh. Not only is their flesh outstanding but also their fur. The small plants on the Warren and the short fine grass produces beautiful, fine, small hair'. At that time they fetched 9s. 6d. a dozen in London between 'Bartholomew and Michaelmas', and 10s. 6d. from then till Christmas. Rabbits and pigeons, of course, formed an important part of the winter diet when many cattle had been killed off. As for numbers, Mr Gilbert reckoned that the 8,000 kept in stock increased annually to 24,000.

When Thomas Walrond farmed the rabbits in the fifteenth century he agreed to reduce their number by 1,000 at the desire of the tenants. You will be lucky today if you see two or three, and I wonder what Aubrey, the Professor, or Mr Gilbert would have said had they walked on the Chase in 1955 and seen, instead of the 'best and sweetest and fattest rabbits in England', unrecognisable little creatures, swollen, blind, deaf—understandable perhaps but very sad all the same. Many villagers still remember with regret the loss of the rabbits, which, they say, really excelled any they had ever tasted.

TWO

War, Peace, and Dissent

WAR

I spoke in 'The Chase' of the 'riotous tumulting' in 1643, and of how later in that same year men with a far different purpose gathered there. Civil War was tearing England apart. The Earl of Essex hastened towards London after the relief of Gloucester. Rubert, well primed, set out from Oxford with 5,000 men to intercept him.

Henry Foote, sergeant in the Parliament Horse, tells his own story of the ensuing battle, in a far more personal way than Clarendon. 'On the Sabbath Day' (September 17) 'we marched from Cricklet to a market town called Swindown . . . This morning news was brought that the Cavaliers were come to Cicester and had taken and killed many of our men . . . This night our London Brigade was quartered at a little poore village called Chiselton, where we could get no meat or drink but what we brought in our knapsacks; most of us quartered in the open field, it being a very cold frosty night'.

As soon as day dawned these tired, shivering men moved on 'to a place called Abern Chace. Here our Lord General made a stand in a deep valley' (the Dean, round Lower Lodge Barn) whence they saw a great body of horsemen gathered round Duddon Lodge, scene of so many poaching affrays. A small force went up to meet them but were driven down the steep hillside. Essex, recognising the hopelessness of his position, ordered a retreat into Aldbourne itself. The Cavaliers followed, firing fiercely the whole way. 'We fired some Drakes at their Horse,' continues Foote, 'but did little execution . . . Col. Hervice's troops drew up in a body and gave the enemy a very fierce charge, which was performed with as brave courage as ever men did . . . One man of great note and esteem of the enemie's partie was here slaine, Marquess de la Vad, his father a Lord High Marshall of France . . . we took up his body and carried it to Hungerford.'

This was the Marquis of St Vieu Ville, who had attended Queen Henrietta from Holland and joined the Royalist army; destined to die in the service of a King not his own and to be buried in a small remote English town. Lord Jermyn, shot in the arm, owed his life to 'the excellence of his armour', and Lord Digby was temporarily blinded by a shot in the face. 'This', says Clarendon, 'may be reckoned one of those escapes which that gallant person hath passed in greater number than any I know'.

During their hasty retreat through the village, two of the Parliament ammunition waggons overturned and were blown up to prevent their falling into Royalist hands. Exhausted, and incapable of further resistance, the sad little army made its way to Hungerford, shelled by the enemy as they went (when the new road from Swindon to Hungerford was being dug some 60 bodies were found near Crowood). Henry Foote tells how, wet to the skin, the Cromwellians quartered that night at Chilton Foliat. But Aldbourne had not seen the last of the warring troops. In May of the following year, after a Parliament force had captured Malmesbury, 15 miles to the north, they marched on Aldbourne, and left some 300 of their horsemen there; pretty certainly, according to their custom, lodged in the Church. That was no doubt when Thomas Goddard and his family, kneeling in the south aisle, lost their fingers. A troop of Royalist cavalry galloped down and captured 17 prisoners, but promptly released them in exchange for horses; a very common-sense transaction.

This seems to be the last fighting in Aldbourne, though in the previous month a muster of the Royalists, 5,000 foot and 4,000 horse strong, with another regiment of horse from Marlborough, had assembled on The Chase, ready to engage two Parliament armies advancing on London. But this time there was no fighting. It may be that cannon were never again heard up there till the First World War, when American soldiers used the old houses at Snap as targets.

One event connected with the outbreak of the Civil War must be mentioned here. The Vicar, Richard Stewart, apprehensive of what lay ahead, carried off the earliest Parish Registers in 1637 for, as he thought, their greater safety. I shall say more of this later.

PEACE

After the Great Muster the Chase settled down to its old way of life, even though it could never be quite the same again. Deer declined rapidly during those disturbed years, when landowners were too preoccupied to attend to them, and they are seldom mentioned after the war. But undisturbed now by the charging of horses and rattle of guns, the conies browsed again on the short, sweet grass, filled many Aldbourne pots, furnished many a London table, and brought a considerable amount of money to the village.

Flocks of sheep feeding on the Chase grew larger—those small-bodied, long-legged, horned sheep which fertilised the lowland fields at night and followed their shepherds up the sheep-walks when daylight came. And down in the village two lots of people, destined to play an important part in its future prosperity, were breeding sons to carry on the two great industries which they themselves started. These were Mary and William Cor, Bell-Founder, and Joan and Edward Witts, Fustian manufacturer.

After all the dislocation caused by the War personal dissensions must have been inevitable, and religious dissention grew. But prosperity steadily increased and with it Aldbourne's reputation as an important place. A steady succession of industries did much to build this up.

DISSENT AND A CENTENARIAN

When Richard Stewart left the village Puritanism was growing fast. In Marlborough, the town with which its relations were closest, Puritans had been preaching regularly since the beginning of the seventeenth century. Among Aldbourne Puritans William Wild is an outstanding figure, because, according to his own account, he lived to be 116 years of age. In the village is a portrait—a really well painted one, though by an unknown artist—of him when he was 106, and because he was drawing large crowds to hear him preach in 1638. If he indeed reached that remarkable age he qualifies, according to the *Guinness Book of Records*, to be the oldest Englishman to date, though one old lady seems now to be competing with him.

Sad to say, since we all love records, Richard Stewart, when he took away the early Parish Registers, also robbed us of our only possible means of establishing beyond doubt the truth of Wild's claim. All the same it seems likely that the Vicar who buried him in 1706 sufficiently satisfied himself by facts provided by the old man before he wrote, 'William Wild was born in ye yeare 1590. d.—ye hundred and sixteenth yeare of his age'. Certainly in his portrait William looks fit to live another ten years. His rugged face is singularly unlined, his eyes shrewd and penetrating as though still able to detect the evil in mens' hearts. And he still has abundant hair, clipped away on his face to show his powerful jaw. Small wonder if he looks a little grim, considering all the persecution he must have suffered. He belonged to an old village family who owned a piece of land called 'Wilds', according to an assessment for Church Repairs in 1795.

It seems that Thomas Wild, buried in 1639, was his father. Also it is amusing and not unreasonable to identify his grandfather with the John Wyld caught poaching in the Chase in 1528 by William Waldrond, Constable of Aldbourne. This story is told in *The History of the Waldronds* (R. W. Waldrond). After words between them, John 'drew a woodknyff upon the sayd William Waldrond and struck him on his nake and upon his hed, whereas the sayd William

Waldrond had no sword nor woodknyff upon him but his fyst where-wyth he defendyd hym and struck the same Jn. Wyld'.

The man in the portrait could so well have inherited his ancestor's combative spirit, if not his violence. The portrait suggests a tough character with the power to survive hard times. The revolt against the Anglican Church, which Wild helped to pioneer, continued to grow, till in 1669 some 300 Dissenters were meeting twice a week outside Court House to hear sermons by ejected preachers.

They are dismissed in the Episcopal Returns for that year as being 'Townspeople and strangers, some Gentry', but mostly as 'ye meane people'. Yet in a Census taken by the Bishop of London in 1676 only 328 Dissenters appear as against 782 Anglicans. No doubt many Dissenters preferred not to declare themselves, for though some tolerance was shown for natives of the village, since a local Presbyterian was given a licence to hold meetings in his house, there was none for outsiders.

In 1673 Robert Rogers, a clerk of Hungerford, was fined £25 for preaching twice at Conventicles' in Aldbourne. And then there was stout-hearted Noah Webb, who rode 40 miles every week for three quarters of the year to preach there. He was fined first £30, then £40, but because he had fled some of those present were fined in his place.

THREE

Village Industries

THE BELLS

THE word bells holds magic for all who know and love the village, and for mere passers-by too. One woman, on a long tramp over the downs, listened to them and thought, 'A good place to live in'. After many vicissitudes, she settled there 50 years later. These bells, cast in E flat minor, have rung out from St Michael's Church for over 460 years, not only over the village, but audible across the downs, given the right wind, as far away as Liddington Castle to the north or the Lambourn downs to the east. The Foundry, where six out of the eight were cast, brought work, a reasonable amount of money, and fame for some 150 years; pride and pleasure always.

Exactly why the Foundry started here is hard to say, but a belief exists that the position of the village provided unusually good acoustics. Certainly a garden east of the church possesses a lovely echo of its own: so clearly is the sound thrown back against the steep bank when the east wind blows that the owner assured herself that it must come from some unknown church. Later she realised she had bought an echo as well as a cottage. It is known that bells from other foundries were sometimes brought to Aldbourne to be tuned.

And now for something of the history of this famous foundry; of the bells cast there and of the men who started and kept it going. In 1699 William Cor (earliest spelling 'Cur', then 'Curr' or 'Corr'), helped by his brother Robert, established it in a major capacity at Court House. But nearly 30 years earlier there is a record of 13s. 4d. being paid to 'Cor of Aldbourne for casting of brasses and for the new metal added'. These would be the horse-brasses then so widely used, a line vigorously pursued by later Cors. And long, long before church bells rang they made music over the downs from the neck of sheep. Indeed, there is a pleasant, if not wholly convincing, notion that the word 'bell' derives from the verb 'belare' signifying the bleating of sheep. The Cors made a great number of both sheep- and cattle-bells, as did also the local blacksmiths who occupied so important a place in Aldbourne life. One still does so.

Three different kinds of bells existed. These were a wide cannister-mouthed bell, the Clacket, with its crown slightly wider than its mouth; the Latton, so called from the metal that was used, for house-bells; and finally, the Rumbler, closely related to the Ancient Crotal; strongest of all, its clapper enclosed in a heavy frame, sometimes very big, sometimes no larger than a grapefruit. Its resounding voice made the Rumbler especially valuable for pack and wagon-horses, and gave good warning where lanes were narrow and winding. Often the bells were set to a spring attached to the 'hames', curved pieces of wood or metal attached to a great leather collar (collar-makers occur often in Aldbourne records). The Cors' successors, the Wells, specialised in these Rumblers*. Later, as roads improved and demand lessened, shepherds appropriated them. At Reading Rural Museum you can see two fine sets. But here our oldest bell, cast before their time, must come into the picture.

In 1460 Richard Goddard, from Upham Manor high on the downs, helped to give to the church its fine tower. Twenty-eight years later he presented the Tenor bell, which bears a long Latin inscription. Translated, it runs—'The voice of Michael's Bell tolls from the sky. God be merciful to the souls of Richard Goddard, formerly of Upham, of Elizabeth and Elizabeth his wives, and the souls of all their children and their parents, who caused this bell to be made in the year of our Lord 1516'. This inscription revealed for the first time Richard's double marriage.

There are two especially interesting things about the Goddard bell, cast at Knight's Reading Foundry, and weighing 19 cwt. First it is the oldest in Wiltshire; secondly it bears the arms of a Benedictine monastery at Chertsey, Surrey, i.e., two St Paul's swords crossed by two St Peter's keys. The Monastery went through bad days, till Edgar the Peaceable, great conciliator of the Danes, bringer of law and order to a troubled land, reformed it. The intringuing problem is this: why were their arms engraved on this Aldbourne bell? It is true that monks did cast bells in early times, but though a patent roll of their property in 1610 mentions a dove-cot, a fishery, and other possessions, there is no reference to a foundry. According to Dr Tyssen (in his *Church Bells of Sussex*, 1914) the use of the monastery arms on a few other bells besides their own (one hangs in Chertsey Church), may be because they gave a founder named John White, whose name occurs in the Church-wardens' Accounts for St Lawrence's, Reading, their permission so to do. The Wokingham foundry was working busily as early as the last quarter of the fourteenth century before it moved to Reading in 1493. A bell cast there in 1383 is at Dorchester (Oxon).

Here it seems relevant to note that a William Wells acted as manager at Reading during the first half of the sixteenth century

---

*Devizes Museum has two examples; a big one cast by Robert Wells and a small by John Stares.

and that a John Wells was a foreman in 1578. The Wells, it will be remembered, succeeded the Cors, and more will be said of them later. Another early bell, No. 4, was cast in 1617 at the famous and older foundry than Aldbourne, that at Salisbury. It is inscribed 'Humphrey Symsin gave XX pound to bi this bell. And ye Parish gave XX pound more to make this bell gooe well'—their wish has been amply justified. Because our earliest Registers are missing, Humphrey must remain an unknown personage.

And now, the Cors come firmly back. The blaze of their fires above the village at Court House warmed hearts and hands alike, and the sight of big wagons drawn by horse or oxen with bells on their collars, bearing a load of far larger ones, as they wound down Crooked Corner and across the Green, must have been a familiar and welcome sight and sound. From Court House, and from Bell Court, the Cors sent out not less than 88 bells. Traces of the pits they used are still visible, and so is the deep well that provided the water so essential to casting. The earliest of Cor bells went north to Berwick Bassett, and the next westwards for St. Mary's, Devizes. Others found their way to East Kennet, Rowde, Ham, and Amesbury. The last of all, a 'Priest's bell', hangs in the massive tower of Great Bedwyn. The Cors cast their first bell for their own church in 1703, No. 5. It was re-cast, being badly cracked, in 1915, and is inscribed 'Richard Scory and Edward Francis C. W. Jackson, Vicar. W. A. Corr'., and is ornamented with a cherub, a shield, a medallion of the Annunciation, a plant, two seated figures, a head wreathed in foliage, and a grotesque face, all of which were reproduced when re-cast. This Vicar was clearly a great bell-lover. Another bell, No. 3, put up in 1709, was paid for by money he had collected, partly by a Bell Fair and a 'Boot Fair'.

No. 5 bell shows what craftsmen the Cors were, in design as well as workmanship. Equal richness occurs on several other bells. Their favourite choice was an oak-leaf, for the Cors, unlike the Witts, Fustian makers, were—if I dare risk a pun—English to the core, and had been part of the village long before they set up their foundry. Of all their designs, perhaps none is more fascinating for Aldbourne than a small bird, unmistakably a dabchick. This use shows their close involvement in village life. It does not embellish any of their church bells as far as I know, but is engraved on a rumbler in the belfry, on another found in Court House, on one in Salisbury Museum, and on many sheep bells.

The amount of property once bearing the name of Cor testifies to their prosperity and importance. In a deed of 1852, we find 'Cur's Meadow, Yard and Barn.' This barn, probably the second oldest in the village, is beautiful both within and without. The original William, or maybe his father, probably inhabited 'Cur's Farmhouse', changed later, rather regrettably, to 'Rose Cottage'. But rose or no rose, it remains a delight to the eye, with its well-weathered stone walls, its gables, it re-tiled roof, its mounting block. Other Cor properties included Gibbs'; also Hatts, with a fine barn, later burned down, named Kings Barn, situated in High Town. It was in 1694 that the Cors moved up to 'a messuage and tenement called Court House in Aldbourne with the backside garden and close upland thereto adjoining the Pigeon House thereon'; so described by Oliver Corr in his Will.

They were already small capitalists. In 1686, before they started their foundry at Court House, Allen Cor left a house with three bedrooms, parlour, buttery, a yard with a cow in it, and 'a roll of wood'; probably Cor's Farmhouse. In 1714 John left his personal estate to his son William with directions that he should maintain his (John's), loving wife for the rest of her life; also that she should have 'half the apples that grow in my orchard' and 'the use of the goods in my Loft Chamber', which included that essential to the good life, a feather bed. Like other bell-founders the Cors ran a subsidiary trade, button-making. In the garden of Court House button-moulds were found a few years ago, and in 1850 when the roof was under repair the Vicar, for Court House had now become the Vicarage, discovered several beautifully carved wooden buttons.

After nearly 50 years the Cor business declined, but when their affairs got into a muddled state they still could afford a special Act of Parliament, in 1739, to straighten them out. Two years later their Foundry was taken over by John Stares and then by Edward Read, who between them turned out 100 bells.

The last and most prolific of all the Aldbourne Bell Founders were the Wells family. They took over the foundry at Court House in 1760 and another, whose exact date is not fully established, at a smaller house down at Bell Court. Before being forced to close down in 1826, they cast close on 200 bells. Work on some of them went on at a little foundry on Baydon Hill; others were cast in the garden of Pond House, where the pits in use were clearly visible a short while ago. Robert Wells was a masterly advertiser. The *Marlborough Times* printed this, 'At the Bell Foundry at Aldbourne bells are cast in a most elegant and as musical a manner as any in the kingdom, the Founder having made the theory of Sound as well as the nature of Metal his chief study; also hangs the same, finding all the material in a complete and concise manner. And also Hand-bells, prepared and strictly in tune in any Key, Horse-bells, Clock and Room Bells, the neatest of their several Kinds. Likewise Mill Brasses cast and sold at the Lowest Prices. All orders will be observed by Rob. Wells, Founder, He gives Ready Money and the Best Prices for Bell Metal'. The reference to Mill Brasses brings to mind the beautiful little Wells Brass found on Windmill Hill.

No. 1 bell in Aldbourne belfry is inscribed 'The Gift of Jos Pizzie and William Gwynne. Music and Singing we like so well and for that reason we gave this bell'. Robert Wells himself presented No. 2. According to a story handed down from father to son these two additions to the belfry, in pursuance of an old custom, were set upside down outside the Blue Boar and filled with beer free for all to drink their health.

Robert sent many bells over Salisbury Plain into Hampshire, including Winchester Cathedral, Nether and Over Wallop, Lymington, Andover and Longparish. And to St Thomas, Salisbury, went a peal of eight. Like the Cors the Wells loved to decorate their bells with cherubs and cupids and other designs copied from old brass ornaments that came into their possession when they bought up old metal, and they often added little ryhmes such as one on a Trowbridge bell,

'May all I summon to the grave
the blessing of a well-spent life receive.'

Few Wiltshire churches are without a Wells or Cor bell, and many villages possess a set of their hand-bells. It is worth noting that when an old house was being pulled down here in 1854, a small hand-bell of Flemish origin, dated 1560, was found among the ruins, to help prove the age of this custom.

Many were the special occasions when St Michael's bells rang gaily over the countryside, or slowly tolled for deaths. The Church-wardens' accounts for 1763 contain reference to payments of 6s. 'for ringing His Majestie's Birthday', for 'Gunpoweder Treason', and 'The Birth of a Prince'. In 1818 the sexton received 3s. when he tolled the death of poor little Princess Charlotte in childbirth, for her mother next year and for George I in 1820.

After a long prosperous period, made still more prosperous by the growing popularity of change-ringing, the Foundry started to go downhill about 1812 and in 1826 James, last of the Wells Founders, went bankrupt. It was a sad day for the village when he sold the business to Mears of Whitechapel. Particulars of the sale of his property show how his family had flourished in the past. These include not only Court House and Bell Court but also another small foundry on the south side of Castle Street, together with four cottages; and on the north side, a house, a Weaver's shop and a warehouse.

There was one pleasant event to record when the Foundry closed. With some bells and much material there went to Whitechapel the Wells' coachman, named Kimber, member of an old village family, and his two sons. One of them, Thomas, had worked at Aldbourne as a bell-moulder, and when he joined Mear's Foundry (now Mears and Stainbank) he found himself inspired by the beautiful lettering on many bells that came in for repair or re-casting. Very skilfully he copied them, and put his drawings into four books. They give a valuable record of many bells no longer in existence, and are treasured by the Whitechapel firm. One other interesting point before we leave Mears. They took with them a number of Cor and Wells bells, and when an Aldbourne visitor ran her finger over their surfaces she found the Cor bells to be far smoother, and of finer metal than those cast by the Wells.

One interesting event in the history of the Whitechapel Foundry, the only one in London and dating from 1570, must be recorded here: it cast the famous Liberty Bell which proclaimed the American Declaration of Independence. On this bell is inscribed, 'Thomas Lester of London made me!' Lester being the Master Founder then. Today 2,400 replicas, at a cost of close on £250,000, are being cast at Whitechapel for the U.S.A. where bell-ringing is growing very popular.

I have spoken of the Cors and the Wells purely as Bell-founders. But before they pass from the picture the large part they played in village life is worth noticing. In 1739 Robert Wells signed a presentment 'that the Pond be railed because it is dangerous'. He is also mentioned in 1778–79 as 'Cow-teller', 'Bread Weigher' and 'Ale-Taster'; also as Constable and as responsible for the Perambulation of the Manor. Sometimes the Wells were in trouble themselves. Robert was indicted for cutting down three elms on his leasehold estate in Calf Street (Castle Street); and later for the state of his chimney in West Street; James was named in the Parish registers as fathering a bastard son. The Cors, too, served in many capacities and were often churchwardens, constables, overseers.

Though the Foundry has gone the bells remain, and will remain as far as one dares look ahead, not only to call people to church and to celebrate special occasions, but also for long and arduous bouts of change-ringing. In 1837 the first peal of Grandsire triples celebrated Queen Victoria's accession and this has been repeated many times. Though through the years the ringers often refreshed themselves at the Blue Boar, they don't seem to have taken beer up into the belfry, as did their fellows at Bishop Cannings, over the hill. Once, however, they thought to lay up a drink by hiding a casket behind a tombstone. Unfortunately someone spied on them and when they came out the cask had vanished. Sometimes the weather caused difficulties as when in 1809, an especially hard winter, they found the belfry full of snow.

And what would the bells be without the teams of devoted, dedicated ringers who have toiled up those steep stairs Sunday after Sunday, year after year, in bitter weather or summer heat? And here a special testimony must be paid to the present head ringer, now over seventy, who has rung them for more than 50 years. It is in his blood, for both his father and his grandfather were ringers.

Because of his devotion to bells he has trained countless young people to ensure that they may still be heard in the years ahead. His face seems to reflect their harmony.*

THE FUSTIAN TRADE

Some 70 years before William Cobbett halted his horse above Aldbourne and pronounced it a 'decaying place', another distinguished visitor rode through the village. This was Dr Richard Pocock, later Bishop of Ossery, who differed from Cobbett 'as chalk from cheese' (to use the time-honoured description of Wiltshire itself) in appearance, character, and style of writing. Like Cobbett he adored travel and rode an estimated fifty-two thousand miles through Great Britain, Europe and the Middle East. His descriptions of his journeys are as dull as they are valuable.

In 1754 he sailed from Ireland, scene of all his clerical activities, to stay with relatives in Newbury. Then, on his way to visit his brother, the Vicar of Meinal (Mildenhall), he passed through Aldbourne, and noted it disparagingly as 'a large village, called a town. It has no market'. But when, three years later, he came again, he reported, 'They spin cotton for candles, for cotton clothes and stockings, and the carriers go with cotton back and forth to London'. This almost certainly refers to fustian, since there was never any real cotton trade in Aldbourne, except as a necessary part of the stouter material. For this, cotton yarn was an essential import. After all, Pocock was only a casual passer-by, without much local knowledge. 'Stockings' would be his name for the fustian gaiters that were common country wear.

Pocock was 'a man of mild manner and primitive simplicity . . . who, in his carriage and deportment, seems to have contracted something of the Arab character'; solemn, silent, serene. Can one imagine a more intriguing contrast to Cobbett? When he first rode through Aldbourne, perhaps only two servants accompanied him, but on his second visit, as a Bishop, he certainly rode in greater style. A visitor to an inn in Daventry watched 'a cavalcade of horsemen approaching at a gentle trot headed by an elderly chief in clerical attire [Pocock] followed by five servants at distances most geometrically measured, and most precisely maintained, conducting his horde with the phlegmatic patience of a sheik'. As such he in fact appears in a portrait sold at Christie's in 1941, of which the National Portrait Gallery possess a photograph.

We leave this fascinating man, Fellow of the Royal Society, who bathed in the Dead Sea to test a statement by Pliny; climbed

---

*This devoted ringer has now retired both as Sexton (the last that we shall have) and as Bell Master but who will still help to train young ringers. A gay, warm-hearted service in his honour, at which we were allowed to clap, was held.

Vesuvius to test a theory of his own; tried to find the site of Memphis; pioneered Alpine travel (a stone engraved with his name stands near the Mer de Glace)—to pursue his journey to Meinal, and return to his allusion to the Aldbourne cotton trade, undoubtedly the fustian one, flourishing at that time. Though the word is far less inspiring, less evocative, than 'Bells', and though it never brought the same fame to the village, it started earlier, lasted longer, and provided more employment. In fact it became the most important centre in Wiltshire for fustian.

Some may ask 'just what *is* fustian?'-Or, they may remember how Grumio in *The Taming of the Shrew* enquires if the serving men are ready 'in their new fustian and their white stockings'. Pope used the word to describe the work of a minor poet who wrote prose under the guise of poetry. Turning to the Oxford Dictionary, we find it means 'Bombastic, worthless, pretentious', though for many people it simply suggests something coarse and homespun. And this, in fact, describes the material made in Aldbourne for some 150 years. Fustian was a very durable material, with a warp of extra stout linen yarn, spun, it may be, from flax grown in the neighbourhood (Celia Fiennes noted fields of it on the Wilts–Berks borders) and soft-spun, single-thread cotton.

The name derives from Elfustat, a suburb of Cairo, its birthplace. Italy seems to have been the first European country to adopt it, and in a petition to Parliament, during Queen Mary's reign, 'fustian of Naples' is mentioned. But the cloth had been used in England much earlier for priests' robes and womens' dresses. In time a stouter, stronger variety was evolved to meet the needs of both field and iron-workers.

When the value of rubber for water-proofing was still unknown the twilled surface of fustian gave better protection against wind and rain than any material. This quality can be seen in the three-quarter length man's coat at Reading Museum of English Rural Life. Though the surface of the material is fine, almost velvety, it is immensely thick and strong. In spite of its age, probably around 150 years, and its use in village plays in the Stroud area of Gloucestershire after its working life was over, this coat remains in excellent condition. Lined with a second layer of fustian, with immense pockets both inside and out, it must have indeed been a godsend to the man who wore it.

The name covers a wide range of materials, but all of the same ribbed character. A primitive type of loom, with special knives for cutting the fine weft 'picts' was used. In Aldbourne, fustian almost certainly belonged to the variety later known as moleskin. This turned later into the brown corduroy so familiar in the English countryside through the second half of the nineteenth, and the first part of the twentieth century. Indeed, since 'Corduroy' appears as a surname in the Aldbourne registers as early as 1684, it may have been a recognised type of fustian even then. Today the omnipresent 'jean' seems most akin to it. The earliest known mention of fustian in Wiltshire occurs in the Bishop of Salisbury's transcripts when a fustian weaver named Humphrey Godswerne of Sherston acted as bondman for the marriage of John Henry in 1627. But at Aldbourne Edward Witts may well have started making it very nearly as early.

The origin of this notable family has never been fully established, but it seems certain they came from either Holland or Flanders. At Leyden there was a black fustian dyer named Colaert Witt in 1622. Because the Church Registers were taken to France for safety in 1637, fixing any exact date for the Witts' arrival is impossible, but Thomas, probably a brother of Edward, had a daughter baptised in 1646, and Richard was buried in 1659. His widow died of small-pox during an outbreak in the first quarter of the eighteenth century. Edward, king of fustian makers, married Joanne Hinton in 1649, and she gave birth to a son next year. In 1666 Edward issued a trade token bearing his initials and a shuttle. Certainly the industry was going strong by 1688, when Edward died and left in his Will 'fustian pieces in several places £146' and 'fustian and Scotch yearn [perhaps a sidelight on where the cotton came from] in his Chambers, valued at £40', also 'Looms and Work still on them of £40' at his 'Callinder House, adjoyning to the George Inn'.* A cow, a horse, brewing vessels and a 'parcill of wood in the backside', likewise figure in the Will. The George Inn stood at the south-west corner of the Green, and is now the Post Office. Part of it is very old, the floors and walls of immense thickness, and the same is true of the house next door. Edward speaks of fustian pieces 'in several places', and this probably included the house in West Street called Witts House, referred to in a number of deeds, among them a covenant dated 1743.

Edward left his five sons well provided for, but like Jacob of old, he perhaps loved his youngest, Benjamin, best since to him he bequeathed his 'callinder house'. After his death the family continued to dominate the industry, and their name appears almost annually in the registers from the second half of the eighteenth century, with only a short break, well on into the nineteenth. Edward issued his own halfpenny token in 1666 engraved with a shuttle.

Other families, however, became closely linked with fustian, notably the interesting and all-pervasive 'Pizzies', who merit a chapter to themselves. As often happens in such family histories the Witts varied greatly in status as time went on. In 1771 an Edward Witts, who left the village to become a solicitor, re-visted his birth-

---

*Callendering was the name given to a part of the process of producing fustian.

place and wrote a full account, handed on to a descendant, Major-General Witts. This tells how Edward talked for a long time with an old Samuel Witts, 'at that time in a very poor state', one of 13 children. His grandfather seems to have been the Thomas who died in 1685, brother of the first Edward. Samuel remembered hearing that the family came from abroad. 'One [the first Edward] flourished exceedingly' he said, but the other moved to Ramsbury 'and by negligence grew exceeding poor.' Edward Witts went on to chat with another ancient man, Roger Commer, whose wife belonged to a humbler branch of the Witts family. Her father had been apprenticed to the first Edward. Roger perfectly remembered Edward's widow, Joan, and said 'she taught school', after her husband's death from 'a Dead Palsy'. Roger also remembered how Edward was lying dead when William of Orange (not yet crowned) passed through Aldbourne. A most interesting memory, because, in fact, William received King James' Commissioners at the Bear Hotel, Hungerford on 8 December 1688, the day before Edward's death, and afterwards stayed at Littlecote.

Joan Witts, besides teaching, ran the fustian business herself until her eldest son, another Edward, took it over. He was twenty when his father died and left him heir to a flourishing business. And, moreover, an ever-growing one, since in 1709 Aldbourne, 'an ancient market town of the Duchy of Lancaster', petitioned Parliament to make the Kennet navigable to Newbury, and, to add force to its appeal alluded to 'the abundance of poor' employed in making fustian. This request was eventually granted in an Act of 1714. We know that much raw material for the linen industry came by boat from London to Newbury, and no doubt a lot of raw cotton too. It may well be that fustian did actually travel along the Kennet, but Richard Pocock's allusion to it shows that wagons were still kept busy in 1757. As the volume of trade increased a central factory was set up in a brick building, still standing, in the grounds of Yew Tree Cottage, South Street, when the roof was lifted to make more room. But looms continued to work in smaller houses. A London Trade Directory for 1792 lists six fustian manufacturers, including three members of the Pizzy family.

Then, in 1761, disaster overtook the village. A terrible fire swept through it and destroyed not only a great many houses but also whole warehouses full of fustian and of cotton ready for weaving. It may well be this that caused one of the smaller manufacturers, Joshua Shepherd, to go bankrupt that same year, and to become in succession straw-hat maker, brickmaker, hop merchant, and finally chapman, or pedlar. In 1777 a second fire, driven by a wild wind, caused even greater havoc. And, as if this were not enough, the fustian trade faced an unequal struggle with the factories springing up like mushrooms in the North. The sound of its own small looms grew fainter and fainter as the years went on.

In the baptismal registers for 1813–1836 the names of only 11 weavers are recorded and Pigot's Commercial Directory for 1831 has this to say, 'Aldbourne, once of much greater extent and consequence than at this period . . . The manufacture of fustians at one time employed the capital of many respectable residents, but that brand of trade is nearly lost, and the place is fast merging into an obscure village'. Here indeed is an echo of Cobbett. But both he and Mr Pigot proved equally false prophets. They judged the future of Aldbourne from what they saw with their own eyes, or from other people's statistics. But as outsiders they failed to assess the recuperative power of a village so rich in tradition, so fortified, even if unconsciously, by its setting among the downs.

Though Broome Witts is given as 'fustian manufacturer' in 1842, and the Census for 1851 records the names of three women weavers, one 'a drapery weaver' aged eighty-three, the good old days when the carriers went 'back and forth to London' were gone forever. Before the industry finally died several members of the Witts family turned to other industries, or combined them with their own. Edne Witts, an influential person in the life of the parish in the second half of the eighteenth century, is spoken of as a Bell-Founder in 1774. He and his brother Broome (father of the Broome already mentioned) took part in the first Grandsire Triples rung from the Church tower in 1771. A grandson of Edne, also called Edne, displayed on his book-plate a small short-legged, long-beaked bird, almost certainly a dabchick, standing on a shield above three racing hares, too long-legged to be mistaken for the famous conies; they may well represent some coursing interest. Meetings were being held in Aldbourne in 1841, where the Warren still offered much open space. Also the Witts now owned quite a bit of land.

In the 1851 census Broome Witts is recorded as farming 381 acres, and the name is carved on a merestone on the eastern bounds of the village.

Long after the virtual death of the fustian industry, quite a lot of the material survived. A remnant found in the roof of an old house on the Green some 30 years ago testifies to its lasting quality, and an amusing episode further illustrates this. When Charles McEvoy's play, 'The Village Wedding' was to be acted in Aldbourne in 1910, Mrs Mabel Stacey was chosen to make the clothes because her hands exceeded all others in skill, as also did the fertility of her imagination. One of the actresses went to her and asked, 'What be I gwine to wear then?' 'Brown jane', was the reply. 'Brown jane!' cried the outraged girl, 'I wonta wore "un".'

She had expected something pretty, something dainty, and knew 'Brown jane' as common, ugly stuff; in fact as a survival of fustian, to turn later into 'jean'. Charles McEvoy was adamant, rough simplicity must be preserved.

And the last fustian of all protected the hands of Aldbourne hurdle-makers working on the southern bounds of the parish. These men, up till the First World War at all events, wore mittens, or 'cuffs' of fustian bought at Harrison's Drapery Stores in Ramsbury. It seems a far cry from birth under the Egyptian sun to a slow peaceful death in the hazel copses of Wiltshire.

STRAW PLAIT

The last bell had been carried away from Aldbourne, two great fires had destroyed warehouses full of fustian, and northern looms were silencing those in the village. Supplies of linen and cotton depended on horse and wagon, and roads in the early nineteenth century were in a shocking state; vehicles were often held fast in deep chalk ruts on the downs. But all round the village fields produced a fine quality wheat. And though it is true that large flocks of sheep occupied most of the uplands they came down in winter to enrich the soil. And just at this time straw-plait was beginning to be much sought after.

Bedfordshire, especially noted for its wheat was, of course, the home of the industry in England. It is believed to have started round Dunstable and Luton as early as 1680. In 1682 wagons were said to be taking hats to London, and in 1689 hat-makers lodged an appeal on behalf of their industry. In Vol. II of his *Tour Round England* in 1725, Defoe noted its rapid growth in Bedfordshire. Incidentally these dates show the absurdity of William Cobbett's claim in 1825 that he had introduced straw plait into England a few years previously from Italy.

Overseers and Poor Law authorities noted with deep satisfaction the increasing demand for straw plait. Here was an admirable way to help paupers to pay for their own upkeep. Agricultural distress was growing worse every year and there were a large number of unemployed, especially among the elderly. The word 'pauper' appears constantly in the Parish Registers. In 1725 a Bedfordshire Workhouse (Caddington) was supplied with 'hatting straws', and soon afterwards appears a record of the apprenticeship of 'poor children' in the art. Though apparently slow to follow this lead in Wiltshire, the Society for the Betterment of the Poor eventually got busy in the county. In 1801 they sent an instructor to Avebury, who claimed to have 100 women and girls at work in a very short time. Delighted by this success, the Society issued a pamphlet entitled 'Hints on the manufacture of Straw Plait', and Devizes now received an instructor. In six weeks, 50 women and children had been taught 'the whole art of the straw plait', according to the Society's Report, and other villages round, including Aldbourne, soon followed suit. As the demand increased, others than 'the poor' became involved in this new business, especially as trade with the Continent was at a low ebb because of the French wars. Italy had formerly taken foremost place in the supply of quality straw hats.

In Aldbourne, again alert to seize an opportunity, several straw-hat makers started business, including Joshua Shepherd, the bankrupt fustian manufacturer, who appears as such in Pigot's Directory for 1830. Joshua and his fellow employers must certainly have profited by the special straw-plait schools for children which started up in the early nineteenth century in various districts of southern England. There is no record of any particular centre in the village, and probably individual employers supplied straw ready for plaiting to people working at home.

Careful preparation was essential. First the straw must be thoroughly dried in the sun, and only the second upper joints could be used. Next, the 'pipes' (or straws) were cut by a simple tool with a wooden handle, three to five in. long, tipped with an iron cutter shaped like the spokes of a wheel. This was pushed through the straw to give five to eight splits, according to the quality required. Specimens can be seen in Devizes Museum. Then, before the final plaiting, the splits were thoroughly damped, and for a really high-grade plait, treated by sulphur fumes. A small workshop in Lottage existed for doing this. Finally the straw was plaited into squares, and the greater number carried away to London, where they fetched eighteenpence (old coinage) a dozen. But some were made up into hats and bonnets in the village.

The finest squares of all were called 'toscins', from Tuscany, home of the fine straw plait, and were used for fashionable women's headgear. At Reading Rural Museum a number of examples of exquisite quality may be seen. Especially pleasing are those entitled 'brilliants'; bleached and made of the very finest straw, they shimmer like silver. The reverse side, a little less brilliant, shows the 'rice' side of the splint. Another delightful pattern is the 'Eye-lit Cordinet' with a fine intricate loop to the edge; a third has a 'feather edge'. The bonnets and hats made from them would have surpassed anything we are ever likely to see again.

Though these are examples from Luton, we may well believe similar designs were fashioned in Aldbourne, as instructors came to Wiltshire from Bedfordshire. Two different slender straw splitters are shown at the museum, one with five blades, for the finest work, and the other with four.

A coarser type of plait, also there, was used for wide, stout country hats, such as are pictured in rural landscapes of the period, for men and women working out-of-doors still thought it sensible to protect their heads from the sun. Thomas Orchard, busy at his thatching, Joseph Herring minding his sheep on the downs, hurdle-makers in the copses, ploughmen in the fields, would certainly have worn serviceable hats; straw in summer, battered old felt in winter. The coarser plait, too, went for baskets, fire-screens, and table-mats.

Unlike the fustian trade, women and children did the bulk of the work. While it lasted it gave pleasant and reasonably profitable employment, especially if we remember the excessively low agricultural wages then prevailing. Though it is difficult to supply definite dates, it seems that fingers were kept busy for 20 years or more. But the supply of wheat-straw was limited by other demands. In Aldbourne there were, and still are, immense thatched barns, and also a great many thatched cottages; thatched walls too. Also more barley was being grown, and farmers could no longer spare enough of the right straw. And so the industry gradually died; and many well contented plaiters found themselves idle. The sad day came when the last consignment of squares set out for London; the housewives swept up the last litter of straw from their floors; the children, half glad, half sorry, missed the extra pennies in their pockets, but had more time for play.

The Green became once more the scene of the old games, the shouts, the laughter, that had enlivened it from time immemorial; once again the church clock could be heard more clearly ringing out the old tunes such as, 'Songs of Praise that Angels Sing', 'Home Sweet Home', now that the indoor work was over. But again Aldbourne needed to show her ingrained resilience.

THE WILLOW TRADE

Once again Aldbourne people met the challenge presented by the decline of the straw-plait. It so happened that just at the right moment, in 1842, Dolly Varden fluttered out of *Barnaby Rudge* in her saucy little hat trimmed with cherry-coloured ribbon, 'worn the merest trifle on one side—just enough to make the most provoking head-dress that ever malicious milliner devised', to fill the hearts of other young women with a warm desire to imitate her.

No sooner did certain enterprising Aldbourne men learn of this increased demand for fine plait from their newspapers or from gossip in Swindon market, than they looked round for some other source of supply than the good wheat-straw that had once served them well. So their eyes turned from the cornfields to the willows bordering their winter-bourne; more particularly the eyes of William Pizzie, member of an ancient village family, whose name, derived from the Berkshire 'village of Pusey', and spelt in at least four different ways, appears almost annually from 1648 for over 300 years; and of Tom Liddiard, another descendant of an outstanding Aldbourne family.

They, followed by others, evidently set to work without delay, for in 1842 Pigot's Directory enters Pizzie as 'Willow Bonnet Maker', and Tom Liddiard soon had ten men and many women and children working under him. Thirty to 40 looms were kept busy in the village. Pizzie himself lived in Vine Lodge, the trim little Georgian house on the Green next door to the Blue Boar, and much of the work was carried on in a shed here and in neighbouring cottages; two of them are still known as Willow Cottages. According to the 1851 Census 26 willow-weavers lived in this part of the village and William Pizzie employed 92 girls, though only four boys. Perhaps feminine fingers were more agile than male ones but also, of course, boys were in great demand on the farms by the time they were ten years old, for ploughing, sheep-minding and bird-scaring.

But in High Town John Smith, described as 'Willow manufacturer', had his two sons as well as three daughters, aged between 18 and nine, all entered as willow basket-makers. Only Martha, three years old, seems to have been exempt. Altogether 133 willow weavers are listed in the Census for 1851, and possibly the number was still higher when the Dolly Varden craze was at its height. Half a dozen small employers held the monopoly of the trade, and Charles Liddiard, son of Tom, recalled in his old age how they could never satisfy the London dealers in their attempt to keep pace with the unceasing demands of those 'malicious milliners'. These dealers at one time came clamouring into Aldbourne four times a week often to collect direct from the cottages, and, said Tom Liddiard, 'I've often had stray buyers pressing for more squares of plait than I could supply.'

Only two mentions occur of local bonnet-makers. Tradition has it that some willow squares were even exported to the Continent. These squares measured about two ft each way, and fetched, apparently as with the straw plait, eighteenpence a dozen—a grossly inadequate amount, one would think, even at the current value of money. On one occasion at least, an indomitable woman decided to rob the middle-men of their exorbitant profits. This was Tom Liddiard's wife. Off she set to walk the whole 70 miles to London, carrying ten dozen squares on her head direct to the milliners. But on the whole the village seemed well content, especially the women and girls who performed the bulk of the work, leaving the harder part to the men. Mistresses sought for maids in vain in those days, and farmers for women stone-pickers and turnip-pickers and suchlike back-aching jobs.

Willow weaving was light, clean work, and girls could earn as much as eleven shillings a week while it flourished. It brought some £50 weekly into the village. Though the willow has always been traditionally linked with sadness, supposedly because of the 'weeping' variety, no Aldbourne girl would so have thought of it in those days. Maidens deserted by their lovers would not have imitated Barbara, maid to Desdemona's mother, who—

> 'Had a song of willow,
> An old thing it was but it expressed her fortune,
> And she died singing it.'

The children, too, again had money in their pockets, since they began willow-work at six or seven or even earlier, and hawkers would declare that when they knew nowhere else to go their thoughts always turned to Aldbourne.

Alfred Williams, Swindon's railway poet, gave a full account of the willow trade in an article published in the *Wiltshire Gazette* in 1892 on Wiltshire Village Industries. Young willow trees, cut directly the sap began to flow, were peeled and sawn into pieces a yard long. These in their turn were split into quarters, and the quarters shaved finely by hand-planes. The strips were then torn apart into strands even finer than straw, ready for an incredibly fine plait. Anyone who has held a piece in their hands, as I have myself done, will appreciate how delicate it actually was: Reading Rural Museum contains a sample. Probably the first plait, made from the local willows, was of a coarser nature, but in a little while manufacturers started going over the hill to Cricklade and Ashton Keyne for a willow more suited to their need, probably the harder type known as Crack Willow, such as was also used for cricket bats. Aldbourne never actually made those, but according to Charles Liddiard it sent off specially prepared wood to Nottingham on at least one occasion.

The importance given by Victorian housewives to a handsome screen to place in front of their fire-places in summer also helped to keep the looms busy; some of coarser, some of finer plait, according to the status of the home. And also they thought it essential to fill their empty grates with willow shavings. Sometimes these were bleached white, sometimes dyed a bright colour. During the latter half of the nineteenth century as much as five tons of shavings, all neatly tied up in bundles, were driven from Aldbourne. One man reckoned to send out 100 lbs. a day.

An old lady, known to everyone as Auntie Nell, now 100 years of age, remembers how as a child she worked with willow and how her father drove near and far round the countryside, his cart piled high with shavings. Not one bit of the precious wood was wasted.

The young pollarded branches, the peelings, the chips, heated the village bread-ovens, particularly the central and most important one behind the present forge, where housewives could get their bread baked for twopence. Possibly some of the waste went to neighbouring charcoal-burners. In such a coal-less county as Wiltshire charcoal would be doubly valuable for heating stoves, and it also served a grimmer purpose, the manufacture of gun-powder. From this arose the old saying that the willows along the Upper Thames fought for the King during the Napoleonic wars.

But gradually industrial changes, as well as vagaries in fashion, killed Aldbourne's willow trade; probably during the last quarter of the century. Young women ceased to tempt young men with Dolly Varden hats, and the introduction of the Panama dealt the industry another hard blow. Also London milliners invented a paper substitute for willow; a far cheaper material, though when it rained the effect was disastrous, and this helped to discredit the genuine as well as the spurious article. In 1867 only two willow manufacturers are given in Pigot's Directory.

Then the gipsies arrived on the scene to destroy the shavings side of the industry. From their caravans and tents behind the Shepherd's Rest, under Peaks' Hill, out from Sound Bottom, they went from door to door with their dyed-paper shavings. The sale of willow shavings rapidly sank and soon stopped altogether. The Pizzies, the Liddiards, the Palmers, the Smiths, who had invested in additional looms when the willow was at its most popular, now found them good only for firewood, and trees that had once fetched 3s. 6d. a foot, were now worth only eighteenpence.

But for some 50 years willow had brought wealth and happiness to the village, and still a few old people recall the talk they heard of it from their fathers when they were young. And even more interesting, an old inhabitant possesses a perfect specimen of willow-work— a delicate little basket of almost lace-like texture—and she also recalls how her eldest sister wore a willow hat for her wedding: 'Lovely it was. All different shades of green. All the girls were trying it on and wishing they could have one like it.'

Another old inhabitant remembers watching his grandfather splitting willow wood for hats or baskets in his garden at Mow Cop.

CHAIR MAKING

After the Bell Foundry had left the village, when straw-plait was on the wane, and because the willow-trade employed a large number of women, but only a few men, Thomas Orchard, woodman and member of a family of woodmen and thatchers, cast an appraising eye on the wealth of trees in the neighbourhood. He realised too, that even cottage people were growing more comfort-conscious, less easily content with wooden benches. Good solid chairs made on the spot provided the answer. Though he is still given in the 1851 Census as 'woodman', and did not actually set up business till 1854, it is probable that two members of the Palmer family, already making chairs in Castle Street, worked under his direction. Four years later he was carrying on a prosperous business at Glebe Farm, in a big thatched barn and yard where One Ash now stands. In

Castle Street, Alfred Bray, his collaborator, who lived at Barn House, thatched in those days, prepared the wood in a large saw-pit in a nearby yard. One man stood in the pit on top of a great elm stump holding a piece of wood steady while another cut it into convenient lengths. Elms came from the Chase, beeches from Savernake, birches from the Woodlands. Orchard himself went round selecting his trees and setting his mark on them. As the branches were sawn through they were lowered gently by a special device straight on to a long wagon known as a 'Timber Bob'. The trunk itself was left to mature on the ground for six months.

The seats of the chairs and their wide back-pieces were of elm, the legs and stretchers of birch or beech; occasionally cherry-wood was used. Once one of the leading workmen chose a specially good piece, and stored it away to make an armchair for the first of his grandsons to marry. This chair was duly made when the right occasion arrived. For cutting the wood into convenient lengths an ingenious lathe was attached by a cord to a pole running along the ceiling of the barn; something that Orchard himself devised. A typical chair had five curved back-pieces, an armchair, seven. A band-saw aided by an iron 'dog' cut the seats, which were afterwards adzed and hollowed for greater comfort. All parts were dried in a heated room and then seasoned in open sheds.

Aldbourne people, with an eye for quality, greatly prized their chairs, and a customary present from bridegroom to bride was four chairs, one with shorter legs for the wife when she nursed a baby, and an armchair. To these Thomas Orchard liked to add a little stool for the mother's feet. Beautifully designed little armchairs for small children were also made. In 1910 the full-sized chairs sold at what seems now the absurdly low price of 18s. for six. Sometimes special chairs were designed to suit special people, as when a huge man, weighing 23 stone, ordered an unusually large one. Small tables were also occasionally made. Many Aldbourne people are still good walkers, but none could emulate Thomas Orchard, who once carried six chairs on his back to Swindon and thereby helped to start the Morse furniture shop.

No wood was wasted. The shavings were a valued by-product; piled into sacks, five to six ft high, they were carried away to innumerable homes for miles around, to heat boilers and bread-ovens, and to start up the open fires universal at that time. This delivery always took place on Saturdays when the farm horses—for Thomas Orchard ran the Glebe Farm as well as his chair business— could best be spared. After some 60 years the business began to decline, owing to the far more mechanised industry at High Wycombe. When invited to link up with them Orchard declined. He was interested only in his own hand-made chairs, as well he and Alfred Bray might be. Some of their chairs still stand, strong and handsome, in many village homes today.

HURDLE MAKING

This seems to be Aldbourne's oldest industry. In so rich a sheep country hurdles were always in demand, and there is a record of them as early as 1295. Hurdle-makers have been kept busy through succeeding centuries well into the present. Several, with us still, remember how they went up into the wood as soon as they left school. One, who belongs to the third generation of men so employed, recalls driving up with his grandfather in a pony trap to the woods early each morning. Later, he and his mates footed it all the way to hazel copses above Pentico, wearing fustian mittens or 'cuffs' to protect their hands. The copses provided a pleasant, peaceful place for working in, and the boys developed a keen eye for birds, far more numerous then than now; among them chaffinches, bullfinches, tits, warblers, jays and magpies. Once a strange bird with a formidable beak and raucous cry appeared for a brief spell. Undoubtedly it was a nutcracker, migrant from Northern Europe, which has since made another visit to Aldbourne. Pheasants abounded, and on these keepers kept a wary eye and would come to drive them away in case of poaching. But no one felt tempted; it would have been as much as their job was worth.

Then, too, there were stoats, weasels, foxes, and—less welcome—rabbits, who multiplied early this century. The hurdlers arrived in the mornings sometimes to find the hazel stems so gnawn away that the stools perished. When the hurdles lay stacked in tens of dozens, along came the farmers' carts, drawn by three or even four horses, to carry them off. In 1910, 6 ft-hurdles fetched only 9s. a dozen, and even less when agricultural depression was at its worst. In the 'nineties my informant's father was driven to leave his hurdles for work in London on the Great Western Railway, but with better times he returned as wood merchant and hurdle-maker. In bad weather the men made sheep cradles down in the village, some of which are still to be found up on the downs. All the waste from the hazels went to heat coppers and bread-ovens, and when a toll of 6d, was still in force at Preston the carters devised a way to avoid payment on more than one journey by chucking their loads over the gate and picking them all up later for only one toll. No hurdles are made here now, and the sheep are usually penned in with large bales of straw stacked one on top of another.

BRICK MAKING

Bricks, we know, were being made here in 1767, when John Shepherd, a fustian manufacturer, went bankrupt and turned to bricks. Where he made them we don't know. It may have been at the kiln up at Love's Copse, on the Ramsbury borders. Another one, closely connected with Aldbourne, was at work on the Woodlands road, beside the inn called the 'Brick-layers Arms', or, more popularly for some unknown reason, 'The Scrubby Cat'. In 1851 two brick-makers each employed two men. Though but a small industry the bricks were said to be of exceptional quality, and were always marked on their underside with a particular 'frog', or small depression, to show where they came from.

THE VILLAGE FORGE

The Forge has always been important in village life and no less than four smiths were kept busy in the mid-nineteenth century. 'Billie' Aldridge, still worked at his forge in Back Lane in 1932 when 81 years old. Shoeing, by appointment, was from 4 a.m. to 7 p.m. daily. An old inhabitant tells how, as a young man due at the Forge at 4 a.m., he overslept, had to fetch a horse a mile away, and arrived an hour late. Billie looked him straight in the face and said, 'Awake thou that sleepest, and wake from the dead, and Christ will give thee light'. A stern lecture followed, followed by a confession that when young he often himself overslept. The racing world knew Aldridge well, and in 1923 he shod the Derby winner Felstead. Every morning during the racing season he walked five miles to Lambourn to shoe the horses, and often was on top of the hill by 4.30 a.m. He was a master at his art, and understood well how to manage even the most difficult animals. Another smith, Fred Liddiard, told how, single-handed, he had completely shod as many as nine horses in a day; oxen too, right up to 1917. The shoes were made in two parts, with inside clips to keep the two halves of their feet apart. Another noted smith was Joe Barnes, who received a handsome certificate from the Worshipful Company of Farriers as a mark of his efficiency.

MALTING

Malting went on in at least three places. Two have been already mentioned, the big barn crowned by its maltster weather-vane, and the other behind Bay House, also very old, as its timbers testified when it was pulled down some 40 years ago. A third occurs in the Enclosure Act at Grazells on, or close to, the site of Beech Knowle where also, in the seventeenth century, stood an inn. Good barley-country naturally gave rise to a considerable amount of local brewing, and even up to early in the present century a few people gathered the wild hops that flourished round Stock Lane.

THATCHING

In a village so full of old cottages, surrounded by cornfields, thatching was an all-the-year-round job, and two men never lacked employment, using the best wheat-straw, and full of pride in their work. Unaccountably, no boys today want to learn the art, while wheat straw is hard to get. The last village thatcher retired a year or two ago, and the nearest one, at Wanborough, can never keep pace with all that is required of him. Both he and his Aldbourne predecessor do, and have done, work of which they may justly be proud.

THE RACING STABLES

For close on 80 years Aldbourne had its racing stables. Horses were being trained at Ford Farm at least by 1898, others at the Old Rectory and at the Hightown stables. These last were burnt down in 1921, and someone vividly remembers how she watched the thatch falling in blazing masses to the ground, and with what difficulty the terrified horses were brought out. Three years later the stables were re-built, and a new owner took over with only a few horses; their number rose rapidly to 30 and later to about 60. Hightown soon became well-known in the racing world, and several famous owners trained there, including Gordon Selfridge and his daughter, Princess Wiasensky. Successes included the Lincoln Cup, and second place in both the English and Welsh Grand Nationals; the latter on 'Ruddimore'. Steeplechasing played a more important part than flat-racing. The head jockey's favourite was Camp Bed. He himself rode a military mule in his early days, once all the way from Gloucester to Cricklade.

The Aldbourne gallops lay on Peke's Down, but horses also trained near Four Barrows, on Russley Down and at Weathercock, opposite Ashdown House. These gallops were considered the best in England; excellent sheep-cropped turf and wide open spaces. It was the custom of the jockeys to feed their horses on the Green as they came out from Hightown, to the indignation of some members of the Parish Council. A resolution forbade the practice, but, said the head jockey, 'We didn't pay any heed'. Eventually, however, they were made to 'pay heed', but most of the villagers saw no objection. The horses, setting off not later than 6 a.m. for Peke's or for their other training grounds, were a popular sight. Of course many villagers laid a shilling or two on a horse, but that side of racing was far smaller, far less commercialised, than it is today.

One old bookie travelled round the village on his flat feet and combined this activity with hair-cutting. He could often be seen at work on a man's head in a yard or garden, often with the aid of a pudding basin. The proprietor of the stables was a kindly man, seldom heard to swear, considerate both to his men and to his horses. He was far too fond of them, said those who worked for him, ever to have permitted the doping which brought the business to a sad end.

Of three living former jockeys one, standing patient and

courteous behind the Post Office counter, loves to fling his legs over a horse whenever he can; another tends horses and occasionally rides over the downs; Paddy Gilligan, father of the present Clerk to the Parish Council, taught Gordon Richards to ride. Sir Gordon reckoned him the best stableman he ever knew. Paddy himself was a proficient National Hunt jockey.

DEW PONDS

One of the most fascinating of Aldbourne past industries was dew-pond making, most closely knit with the name of William Walters, whose tombstone in Aldbourne, dated 1940, is inscribed 'The last of a long line of dew-pond makers'. A just claim since his family made dew-ponds for at least four generations.

First a word about the way they were made, in Walker's own words, published in the *Swindon Advertiser* in 1933. 'First we digs a hole 25 yds across, saucer-shaped and about 12 ft deep in the middle. Then we puts a layer of clay 6 in. thick right over the bottom, that is beaten down with beaters; hard work 'tis I can tell 'ee, till 'tis only about 3 in. thick. A layer of lime-stone goes on top of that, and then another layer of clay as thick as t'other one. A'ter he's beat down we covers the whole lot with rubble, stones, flint as thick as you like, then fill 'un in with water, The layer at top keeps the feet of the cattle from going through to the bottom, and the lime stops frost from damaging it.' The lime also prevented the penetration of worms. Successive makers altered their methods a little as they learned by experience. Mist and rain, not dew, supplied the water.

When only nine, William watched his father repair a pond up at Greenhill, which he had made 42 years earlier after learning the trade from his mother's father, who also sank many Aldbourne wells. After that William helped his father till, at 21, he set up business on his own. Ponds all round Aldbourne, including Hinton, Upper Upham and Liddington, were fashioned by him for 40 years, and he told the reporter, 'I could sit up here and reckon up more than 100 ponds I've made, far and near on the Wiltshire downs'. It was a long and exacting business. A pond at Lillywhites took 13 weeks, with six or seven men to help. A well-made pond cost £80–£100. The very last was on Barbary Castle, made soon after the First World War. In the early days a donkey carried all the workmen's tools, with a barrel of beer slung on each side of him, while the gang rode in a horse and cart. Sometimes they went long distances, once 30 miles away to Castle Eaton in Gloucestershire. They spent their nights in a barn or stayed with the cottagers.

William Walters came of a long-lived and prolific family. His mother's father died at ninety-one and had 11 children; his own father worked on till he was over eighty, and his family also numbered 11. He took an active part all his life in village affairs. In his early days he played in a band of village mummers, and also rang both church and hand-bells. Among his treasured possessions were three walking-sticks which he used to prod the depth of a pond. One, very straight, was of yew from an old tree in the Vicarage garden. The second, all knobs and corners, came from a wild crab tree. The third, most unusual of all, from the stem of a huge sun-flower, 'wi' a fine, silver knob on him, and a vurrell on the back of him'. Not only did William make dew-ponds but he also worked for 40 years at sheep-shearing. 'I sheared 1,000 this year' (1933) he said, 'so if I say 40,000 all told I shan't be vur out'.

A solid grey tombstone is one memorial to him, but better still, for all who walked the downs in the ealier part of the century, are these remote ponds, reflecting the wide sky, full of little water creatures and a few small plants, haunt of certain birds, and above all a drinking-place for thirsty sheep. One by one they have dried up, though a drop of water remains in one on top of Milk Hill, and another near old Shepherd's Shore on the Cannings downs. Piped water is a dull substitute.

FOUR

Agriculture

I HAVE devoted a separate chapter to Agriculture because, though quite the most important industry of all, it is still very much with us and, I hope, always will be. To deal with it adequately would need a volume to itself. Here I shall attempt only a quick look at a few aspects.

SHEEP

As a downland village, sheep have naturally always been well in the foreground at Aldbourne from very early days. Flocks of 1,000 or more on the Manor Farm are recorded for the twelfth to the fifteenth centuries. They remained in the hands of the big land-owners, though portions of downland were set apart for the common flock.

In the late sixteenth century Diana Caswell, at Upper Upham, farmed sheep in a considerable way over part of the Warren and in 'Sheeply Bottom' (now Shipley Bottom); a place where 'sheep-leight', or the right of pasturing sheep existed. Coming on to the seventeenth century John Aubrey in his *Natural History of Wiltshire* had this to say of the sheep on the Chase: 'They are not subject to the shakes which the Dorset sheep are. Our sheep about chalke do never die of the rot. My cousin Scot do assure me that I may modestly allow a thousand sheep to a tything . . . Mr Roger was for allowing of two thousand, but my cousin Scot says that is too high.' He goes on to assert that 'the masters give no wages to their shepherds, but they have the keeping of so many sheep *pro rata*; so that the shepherds' lambs do never miscarry'.

Rather a wide generalisation perhaps. Arthur Young, writing some 100 years later of his ride through Wiltshire (*Annals of Agriculture*) also bears witness to the large flocks round Aldbourne. All the ewes kept for breeding, he said; also that 'the lamb and the wool bring the profit'. Sheep were selling then at about £1. Earlier the wool of Wiltshire sheep was less prized than their manuring of the soil. A sidelight on the price of sheep in the early eighteenth century occurs in an inventory of the goods left to William Liddiard of Aldbourne, in 1709, where 'four score ewes and lambs, and six rams, are valued at £30.

William Cobbett is the third reporter on our sheep. When he came riding over the downs from Swindon in 1826 he commented on the immense flocks he saw going out from their folds; one of tegs, one of wethers, one of lambs, with a shepherd for each. 'The lambs,' said Cobbett, 'were beautiful, short-legged and in every respect what they ought to be.' All had black faces and legs; something new to his companion though not to himself. The extent of the turnip-fields close round delighted him. He had a passion for turnip, whether for human or animal consumption.

In 1839 the Manor farmer bought 420 sheep and sold 655, and in 1845 his stock stood at 1,664. This probably meant at least 3,000 to 4,000 for the whole parish. The 1851 Census records no less than 17 working shepherds. But figures for sheep show a definite falling off in the next 30 years. The steam-plough was busy in Aldbourne by 1878, and corn was superseding the flock. But by the end of the century sheep increased again. This coincided with a period of agricultural depression, when small farmers were going out of business and the big ones breaking up the fields and throwing them open for grazing; as happened at Snap, Hilldrop, and Laines. Wheat and barley declined but more oats were grown.

Among notable sheep-farmers in Wiltshire were the Browns, one of whom still farms at the Manor, the third generation of his branch of the family to do so. Now a fourth generation prepares itself to follow suit. Today, when pigs and cows decline owing to the cost of imported foodstuffs, sheep, enjoying their rightful heritage, are again on the upgrade. So just possibly this might bring back some of those downland flowers that used to gladden us—small scabious, harebells, rock-roses, and all the rest of them.

As I have said earlier, a few of our sheep still wear bells, and perhaps more will do so one day. The Manor Farm owns a fine set, not in use at present. The breeds of sheep that crop, or have cropped, our downs, vary greatly through the ages. The old Wiltshire horned sheep died out during the French wars here as elsewhere. An attempt to increase their weight, and also their length of leg, failed, and the last Wiltshire flock was disbanded in 1819. Southdowns succeeded them, followed by Hampshires. During the first years of the century 200 Cheviots were introduced on the Manor Farm, followed by Rylands and Exmoors. Today the sheep are largely cross breeds; Hampshire Down, Welsh, Leicester and Grey-face.

In earlier centuries our shepherds made long journeys over the downs, including almost certainly the shorter one to Tan Hill Fair. The purchase of 140 ewes at Wilton Fair is recorded for 1838, which meant a walk of 32 miles and a night spent in some sheltered spot; the shepherd lying down with his flock. During the earlier part of the present century the Manor carter drove great sacks of wool to Marlborough market, but now it goes to the Wool Marketing Board which acts as the farmer's selling agent.

A final word must be said about sheep-shearing, which used to keep a far larger number of men, also some women, busy, than is the case today. In early summer the hurdle-makers and woodmen would leave their copses and set off on their cycles in bands of eight or nine and ride long distances, accompanied by a 'Tar Boy' whose business it was to carry a tin of tar and a stick. If a sheep was accidentally 'nicked' up would go a cry of 'Tar Boy!' and he would hasten to apply tar to the cut, as efficacious for a sheep as for a tree. An alternative remedy was wood-ash which, rubbed gently into the wound, both stopped the bleeding and acted as an antiseptic. In this case, the cry was 'Mendin!' A few women used to stand round with dust-pans and brushes to sweep the barn floor and gather up any loose wool.

When the shearers worked at Cowcroft the farmer set up a table made of broom-handles, and the man sorting the wool laid it there and found it easier to pick out the 'belly wool' (the coarser kind) from the rest, and especially from the neck wool, the finest of all. This farmer always chose the younger men to help him personally, because he could understand them better, for broad Wiltshire dialect baffled him. He had previously sheep-farmed in Australia. The men had good country similies of their own; no borrowing of Americanisms. 'Like a toad caught under a harrow' described a difficulty graphically.

These gangs sheared immense numbers of sheep in the early part of this century. There was a custom whereby the latest recruit to the gang provided a supper in winter in his own cottage, with a home-cured ham, often accompanied by home-made wine—mostly beetroot or potato, though parsnip wine was also a favourite for such festive occasions. One woman made a kegful and put it to mature. But when she had gone to bed her husband and son would steal out, put a string round a small can and help themselves. Christmas brought agitated cries from the wife.

'Why, if the keg ain't empty!'

'Must have been that stuff you put in have sent it all up in vapourisation,' replied her husband.

She innocently accepted the explanation.

If hurdlers turned sheep-shearers, shepherds sometimes undertook another kind of shearing in the evenings. One man with a large family welcomed men wanting a hair-cut. 'How much?' asked a customer when it was over. 'Doant 'ee bother 'bout that. Just 'ee give the kids tuppence apiece,' replied the shepherd. Ten of them; quite a costly hair-cut.

It took three men to shear 100 sheep in a day, and the prices paid ran as follows. For 'Grass' sheep; that is white-faced sheep who were meadow-fed and never folded, and with the easiest wool of all for shearing, 45s. per hundred; for the Hampshire Downs, or similar breeds, 50s.; for tegs, whose wool tended to be thicker and tougher, 55s. The sheep were washed at three different places: the Manor sheep at Lower Barn, under Rookwood, in water drawn from a deep well; others in a pool at the foot of the hill behind Bay House; the third place was a meadow at Ford Farm, beside Hodder's Bridge, called 'Sheep-wash Bridge' in an old deed, a good spot when the bourne ran freely. But in the early 'twenties all washing ceased. From the farmers' point of view unwashed wool weighed much heavier, and its natural oil began to be prized.*

A crop much fancied by sheep, and also by bees, was the beautiful sainfoin, once widely grown in and around Aldbourne, but now seen no more except for a stray blossom among other wild flowers. Arthur Young wrote, 'Saintfoin is pretty much cultivated near the Downs; they mow it for hay; get two tons an acre; feed the after-grass with sheep. When it is worn out, which will be from twelve to fifteen years [but others give it only seven] they pare and burn it for turnips, then sow barley, and reckon it should be seven years in tillage before laid again to saintfoin'. One old Aldbourne man remembers beating out the seeds of sainfoin, and of other clovers, with a hand-flail. Bees made a delicious lime-green honey from sainfoin—something I fear we shall never taste again.

Incidentally, while talking of Young, it is worth recalling what he said of farms seven miles east of Marlborough. 'The course is; 1. Turnips. 2. Wheat. 3. Barley. 4. Oats. 5. Clover and Rye.' Grain and the rotation of crops in Aldbourne's four large common fields is far too complicated a subject to deal with here. Those wishing to know more of Wiltshire agriculture through the ages should turn to Vol. IV of the Victoria County History for an excellent and detailed account.

PLOUGHING

Aldbourne possessed some highly skilled ploughmen. One, still alive, won first prize for Wiltshire, and received a beautiful engraved certificate which hangs on his wall. The plough he used was made by the Bedford firm of Howard. On either side of a picture of it you see the houses of two famous Bedford Johns—John Howard, famous prison reformer, and John Bunyan. Another man was awarded a gold medal for 50 years' faithful service; and a third one a ploughing prize for boys. Like older men he ploughed a good straight furrow, but not so all the younger men. One, asked by the head ploughman,
'Why can't 'ee keep a straight furrow?'

---

*I am indebted to William Brown for information about sheep on Manor Farm.

replied, 'Well, yer zee, like that t'will bring us more grub.'
'How d'ye make that out then?'
'Why, the hares 'all break their legs runnin' in and out o' they furrows', was the answer.

The older ploughmen clearly found pleasure in their work, in spite of wind, weather and mud. The rhythmic walk to and fro, to and fro, seems to have given them peace of mind as well as deep affection for their horses, so too, for their oxen. This appeared clearly in a talk with the man, then but a lad, who proudly accompanied the four oxen from the Warren Farm when they were exhibited in London in 1910. 'Their names were Golden and Spark, Cherry and Blossom. Each ox had his special companion,' he said. These were flattering names for such heavy bulky creatures and prove the affection felt for them. They may be seen in the delightful collection of photographs in *A Country Calendar* (by Gordon Winter), though Golden was missing because of a bad foot. These oxen were Long-horned Red Devons and a team always numbered four.

Until the early part of this century oxen had always worked in Aldbourne. Arthur Young noted many as he rode about Wiltshire, but though they were thought good on heavy land he declared six were needed to do the work of four horses. Long before the use of oxen ceased the steam-plough was coming into use. A Baydon farmer was operating one by 1870 and Aldbourne followed not long after. Yet horses were working up to 1959.

CHANDLER'S DRILL

In 1848, Thomas Hicks Chandler, of Stockton, who later farmed for 19 years in Aldbourne at North Farm, after much study and experiment patented a mechanical drill for the distribution of liquid fertilisers, and was rewarded a year later by a silver medal from the Royal Agricultural Society. At the Great Exhibition in 1851, according to the *Devizes Gazette*, 'This excited considerable attention and was highly commended' in a report on agricultural implements shown at the Exhibition. A noted Wiltshire agricultural engineer, Thomas Pepies Reeves of Bratton, son of a village blacksmith, was the maker. At a dinner given in Chandler's honour, the Chairman grew eloquent over the drill. 'He doubted not it would be handed down as a precious heirloom. Swedes and turnips grew where none had grown before, and where they had grown, now they grow the more.'

To demonstrate this another Wiltshire farmer tried Chandler's drill on the poorest land in his neighbourhood, on top of a hill where it had proved impossible to grow any root-crops. But after this he produced there 'the heaviest and most abundant crop of swedes that had ever been known for miles around'. Yet despite all this Thomas Chandler met with much scepticism and apathy from farmers, deeply suspicious of any new invention, for a long while. However, he was a man of immense determination, descendant of a family who migrated to New England in the early seventeenth century for their religious beliefs. But Thomas himself was a devoted Church of England man, and he worked zealously and gave generously to the restoration of St Michael's Church in 1867. His son farmed after him at North Farm and was the man who first discovered what wealth of Roman remains lay buried round his home. The Chandler family—intelligent, hard-working, well-rooted in Wiltshire soil—certainly helped to keep the heart of the village beating soundly.

If the Chandler family and others like them were dedicated men, others less fortunate shared their sense of dedication but with less opportunity for giving it full scope. There is a touching example of a small farmer who pined for a few acres more for his cows. His wife, determined to help him, began taking in washing, and put all the money she earned, in gold sovereigns, into a special hiding-place. Early in the century, 11 acres of land near Four Barrows came up for sale at £10 an acre. Out came sovereigns to the value of £100 and the farmer was a proud and happy man, He was free now from his constant anxiety about how to keep his cows properly fed.

An interesting recent development is the increased growth of Oilseed Rape (*Brassica verolofora*), a crop proving valuable in the manufacture of cattle cake, thereby helping to overcome the expense of imported feedstuffs. Also it can produce a particularly fine oil for use in especially delicate machinery. It has replaced charlock and mustard, and adds much to the beauty of the landscape in spring.

SNAP, WOODSEND AND HILLWOOD

I include these three outlying parts of the parish in the chapter on agriculture because their decline is linked with late nineteenth-century agricultural depression.

Beside a sharp bend in the Marlborough road, not far from Ogbourne Hill, is Woodsend (once 'World's End', when only a rough track led to it and it seemed indeed remote). Take the lane west of the houses at the corner and you drop down a steep, winding lane into the deserted village of Snap; Snape or Snappe in earliest records. The name means a rough, wet bit of land, and at the bottom of a small valley there is often plenty of wetness. On the downs not for away stone curlews call, and badgers have their setts. Once it was a flourishing hamlet, home of some seven families whose menfolk all worked for the farmer. His house, a very old one, stood half way up the lane. The earliest record I have of Snap is in a Survey of the Duchy of Lancaster in 1509, where evidence of residence there appears in the statements, 'Richard Eyre holds the croft and one grove now built upon at Snappe'. A 'Survey of the Use of Common Land' in 1551 says, 'The pke of Snape cont. XX acres of X yeres growth'. In 1626 Henry Martyn left his lands to his two sons including 'a tenement and half a virgate in Snappe', and 'ten acres of pasture land in Snappe, called "the Breach" '. The Parish Registers from 1637 onwards contain records of births, marriages and deaths in Snap. A list of qualified voters from 1833–1852 gives the names of three freeholders—William Deadman, farmer, among them.

According to the 1851 Census, seven cottages were inhabited by 50 persons, of whom 28 were children. This is not surprising since a study of the Parish Registers shows six families bearing large families during the second half of the nineteenth century. In 1812 Jane Bridgman, wife of one of the Bell Founders, turned a thoughtful eye on the children growing up so far from the little schools then available in the main village, and she undertook to pay 3d. a week for the education of every Snap or Woodsend child. The annual amount for the teacher came to around £5 12s. She was the wife of one of the Snap agricultural labourers, and probably taught the children in her own cottage.

In 1855 a bequest by a member of the Brown family living at Lower Upham, combined with help from the National Society, made it possible to build a little school at Woodsend. To this came both Snap and Woodsend children, summoned by a small rumbler bell engraved with the Cor dabchick, which is now in St Michael's belfry. This bell sounded not only for school but for worship on Sunday afternoons.

In a letter to the *Wiltshire Gazette* of 8 October 1925 a man who had grown up in Aldbourne told how, as a youth some 40 years earlier, he had played the harmonium at Woodsend, accompanied by some St Michael's choirboys. The Vicar, J. H. Hodges, drove a few of them there in his pony-trap, and took others on the return journey. The congregation sang in a good broad Wiltshire dialect. When this young man left the village the farmer at Snap, 'an excellent fellow', took his place at the harmonium and paid for its upkeep. W. H. Butler, later Vicar of Aldbourne, was curate in 1902, and he recalled in a letter to the same paper how Snap lies in a little valley all by itself, and how he used to go there along a rough grass road, not much used by that time. This was the track that passes by Lower Barn under Rookwood, still a freehold for rooks, and past Hikler (Highclere) Wood, where a wealth of snowdrops points to the erstwhile existence of a cottage, or possibly two. Snap and Woodsend people always went this way.

Everything suggests a small, happy community. Horses, cows, pigs, hens, bees, were all kept, and also, evidently, a considerable number of sheep, since the farmer employed two shepherds. There was good grassland, some corn, well-kept gardens and apple-trees. A very deep well, now filled in, served the cattle, and the cottagers had their own or shared one with their neighbours. You must walk warily in the undergrowth today as one or two there may still be open.

But Snap was doomed when agricultural depression set in towards the end of the nineteenth century. Intensive farming ceased, a large farmer bought up the village and all the adjacent land, which was now given over largely to sheep. The local farmer departed and the cottages emptied one by one, and tumbled to ruins, as did also the farmhouse. The new owner cared not a jot, and jokingly told how he had suffered a new kind of farm casualty when a heifer fell from a bedroom window and broke her neck. This meant that the decaying roof and upper storey had so filled the lower part of the house that she had managed to reach the next floor. The little school-cum-church disintegrated bit by bit. Mr Bob Wilson of Bishopstone told how sad it was to look in and see, when he and his shepherd passed by with some sheep, hymn-books and prayer-books scattered about decaying pews. Gipsies occupied it for a while, and then, when its condition grew too bad, the stones were sold to an Aldbourne builder. In its heyday in 1859 it was reported as being well attended and the teaching good.

It was during this period of deep depression, when the people of Snap had begun to realise what fate awaited them, that a man met his death as he climbed the hillside from Obgourne. He had been drinking too much, perhaps to drown his sorrows, and had fallen on his face and suffocated. When all other cottages were empty one old couple remained just above the home of the dead man. The husband died, but his widow stayed on alone. She, Rachel Fisher, is still remembered by old inhabitants—tall and handsome, black-haired, deeply furrowed face, wearing a black bonnet tied with crimson ribbons; a grand old woman, everyone said. As a young man, harrowing the ground near her cottage, a man now in his own old age vividly remembers how he saw her standing in her garden gazing at her roses. Always when the post-woman, or boys with bread and groceries, came, there was a cup of tea for them, but much concern was felt for the old woman's lonely state, especially by the owner of Upper Upham who often visited her. Unwillingly she at last allowed herself to be brought down to Aldbourne and installed at Cook's Yard.

'How be gettin' on then?' asked a neighbour.

'I feel so lonesome,' replied Rachel.

'Lonesome? With folk all round you?'

'Aye, but I don't hear the birds singing like what they did up there, nor the foxes barking in the night.'

Little remains now to show what Snap once was except for a

tangle of undergrowth and trees; beeches, ashes, thorns, all grown very tall; a few box bushes marking the old hedges; mounds and loose stones. Rachel's roses have run wild, but in the quietness up there you seem to see her standing among them, last inhabitant of deserted little Snap.

Woodsend must have shared largely in the life of Snap. In 1851 31 people lived there, including the farmer at Leigh Farm and 16 agricultural labourers. Among them was Bobby Fox, bee-keeper, well known all round for his honey, delivered in a small donkey-cart. Once, returning from Aldbourne with a sack of meal for his hens, he stopped in Castle Street and hoisted the sack onto his shoulders.

'What be doing that for then?' asked a passer-by.

''Tis to save the old donk,' replied Bobby.

Hillwood, always 'Hillood' to old inhabitants, was another, still smaller, hamlet that died like Snap when it was bought up by the same large farmer. It lies about two miles west of Aldbourne in the valley below Dudmore Lodge. The Duchy Survey, already referred to, has this to say of it, 'There be within the Chace III copic one called hillwood cont. XVI acres of VII yere's growth'. The Census for 1851 shows George Church as the resident farmer, then aged seventy-three. Two sons helped him and he employed 26 labourers, six of whom boarded in his house. In one of the two cottages lived the carter and his wife, who also worked on the farm; in the other two more labourers and their children, who tramped down to school at Aldbourne. They all drew their water from a well worked by a patient old donkey.

On the adjoining hillside, formerly beautiful with cowslips and the white Meadow Saxifrage, lived a large colony of badgers. Many generations must have bred there to judge from the number of setts. One can well believe that badger sometimes figured on a cottage table when life was hard. As Hillwood fell into ruins there grew up one of those wild little woods, so dear to nature-lovers, so sadly unwelcome to landlords intent on tidying up the countryside. If you wandered into it on an early summer day you grew surprisingly conscious of the smell of lilac, and later of syringa— reminders of those former cottage gardens. Earlier in the year the ground was thick with snowdrops. All was a tangle, dreadful or beautiful according to your point of view, full of birds, especially long-tailed tits. But such places seem doomed. All the old trees have been felled and largely replaced by conifers; cowslips and saxifrage no longer have the freedom of the hillside.

FIVE

The Church

Sometimes it happens that a visitor to a strange village has to ask, 'Where on earth have you hidden your Church?' This would never happen in Aldbourne, so proudly does St Michael's proclaim itself. Mary Magdalene was the patron saint of the original Saxon church which belonged, as we learn from their accounts for 1086–1541, to Amesbury Priory. Domesday, speaking of Aldbourne, says, 'to the Church of the Manor belong two hydes. The land is two caricates held by the priest of the same Church'. No trace now remains but the foundations may lie below the cellars of the present building, and the original dedication continued for a while when it was erected in the twelfth century. Aldbourne Feast has always been held within the octave of Mary Magdalen, and probably started around 1222, when a Council Meeting at Oxford ordered all churches to keep their Saint's Day as feast as well as religious festival.

When you enter through the Norman south door and fine Perpendicular porch your first impression is of light and spaciousness, which beautifully fits its setting among the wide open downs. Though no good stained glass delights the eye, equally none seriously displeases. Fire damaged much of the church in the thirteenth century, and it was rebuilt with no old materials. The capitals of the solid pillars are Early English; the roof of the nave, the aisles and the font are Perpendicular; the pulpit Jacobean. In the Sanctuary the figure of John Stone, Vicar in 1501, lies exquisitely incised in alabaster, clad in alb, stole, maniple, and chasuble. His head rests on a richly embroidered cushion, his left hand holds a chalice, his uplifted right a Latin label which reads, 'Holy God Almighty and Eternal, have mercy upon us'. The Chapel in the north aisle is perhaps the most beautiful part of the church. It was once the Chantry of the Fraternity of the Blessed Virgin Mary of 'Our Lady's Guild', and a brass commemorates its priest, Henry Frekylton, who died in 1588.

When all Chantries were dissolved in 1547–8 Thomas Chaffyn, of the Commissioners concerned, bought the furnishings. These included (as recorded by the Crown Officers in 2. Edward VI) '2 payre of vestments', one being 'of white satten and Bruges [lace] 1 altar cloth, 2 corporasses with case'. These, together with 'a Chalice of silver parcel gilt weighing 12 oz.' were valued at 180s. Even for those days, Chaffyn made a good bargain.

The long, simple lines of Henry Frekylton contrast forcibly with the sturdy Walrond brothers, aged 96 and 84, kneeling close by in fine coloured doublets and broad ruffs, an elaborate monument towering round them. Though they kneel there, they refused to kneel in the body of the church after the Reformation. Edward was fined more than once for non-attendance, according to the Quarter Session Great Rolls. A superscription in three languages describes him as 'a lover of hospitality and entertainer of many friends'. William, having completed an upright life of 84 years, 'entered up on the way of all flesh in 1614. But his body, being reduced to ashes under this monument his soul awaits through Jesus Christ the assumption of a purified body in heaven'. The Walronds lived in the Old Parsonage, burnt down in the great fire of 1771, and were, it is safe to assume, members of the Fraternity.

A tablet in the north aisle commemorates 40 Aldbourne men who died in the First World War.

The burly figure of Thomas Goddard, his meek little wife, Joan, and their family kneel impressively in the south aisle, though slightly humiliated by the loss of fingers. Above hangs Thomas's great iron helmet, weighing at least 8 lb., with removable panels over the face, and fastened behind with hook and eye. Below them lies a brass to another (earlier) Goddard, Richard, who gave the tenor bell in 1480 and helped to build the fine tower in 1460, after it had been burnt down. Unfortunately the pinnacles were never completed. On the south wall, too, are tablets to six members of the Witts family, famous bell founders.

The church's most valuable possession is a silver flagon given in 1678 by Oliver Nicholson, whose marriage to the heiress of Richard Walrond brought him to the village. The design of it, set amid a delicate tangle of foliage, is enchanting, even if entirely alien to its sacred purpose. A chevron is engraved between three owls, another two between three ravens, a 'lion combatant', three bulls' heads and an eagle with outspread wings; all coats-of-arms of important Wiltshire landowners. An engraving of the design can be seen in Devizes Museum. A tablet to Oliver's memory speaks of him as 'Lieut. Governor of His Majesties' Counties of Wilts and Hampshire. Departed this life Dec. 1. A.D. 1683 aged 61'. On the floor of the Tower a stone commemorates his wife Frances.

Two old chests in the Vestry hold the Churchwardens' accounts. In 1792 appears this item, 'Paid for ye Cheaste that was brook 1/6'. Another entry 20 years later reads, 'To the Widow Smith's bill for mending the late destruction of the Church, £5 16s. 5d.', for damage by the great fire in 1760, a remarkably moderate bill. Another entry (1785) for 4s. for 'a pot for ye Chimney over ye Porch'. Naturally through the years many changes have taken place. Once there were galleries at the west end, and in them Thomas Stron of London, belonging to an old village family, put up seats for the Sunday School that he started in 1786. A later entry records damage caused by unruly children amounting to £3 15s. 6d.

In August 1867, after services had been held in the village school for about a year, an extensive restoration of St Michael's—directed by H. Butterfield—was finally completed. Queen Victoria's Jubilee also saw extensive restoration, and since then constant care and attention have kept the church what it is today. The only sad thing is the reblocking of the West window, this time by organ pipes.

At the top of the steep churchyard, a most peaceful spot, is a seat given in memory of Muriel Foster, who loved watching and listening to birds and who encouraged children to do so, too. You can often hear a blackbird singing there.

THE CLOCK

During the restoration that took place in 1887, among many other things the old lozenge-faced clock was changed for a round one, and the four-year old son of the Lord of the Manor was carried howling all the way up to the belfry to set it going. A plaque on the south wall records this event and ends, 'So let us number our days that we may apply our hearts unto wisdom'.

Like the previous clock the new one played hymns three times a day: an old inhabitant remembers going to school to the tune of 'Jesus, meek and mild'. But not all children even in those authoritarian days were meek and mild. The little old schoolmistress taught unruly boys and suffered many kicks. The change of tunes was an elaborate process, and not undertaken more than twice a year. 'Songs of Praise the Angels sang', 'Home Sweet Home', 'Now the day is over', all within the octave, were part of its repertory. To the grief of many old inhabitants the re-hanging of the bells in 1914 silenced the tunes because of labour and replacement difficulties.

Long before the old lozenge-faced clock chimed the hour and tunes, two earlier clocks carried out their task. The Churchwardens' Accounts for 1716 record that William Cor received payment for 'keeping ye Clock and ye chims in order'. In 1775 a new one was installed, but not, apparently, of good quality since it only lasted 12 years. Could the lozenge-faced clock have worked on for a 100 years? It seems it may have done just that.

THE CHURCHWARDENS' ACCOUNTS

Churchwardens' Accounts make fascinating reading, and those for Aldbourne are no exception. They deal with a wide variety of subjects, from 'hear' for hassock to 'men coming out of turkey'. Many items concern seating in church, chiefly in the eighteenth century, as comfort-consciousness increased. Many parishioners installed their own seats; others paid to get the best, among them the Bell-founding Wells family and the Pizzies, for sums ranging between 2s. 6d. to £2 10s. 0d. Robert Church, from the farm up at Hillwood, bought a seat 'of the Widow Blagerough in a Eyle at the north yeand of Mr Martin's seat by paying four pound according to the custom at Enterent'. Frequent items concerning repair of the churchyard occur, and for 'new lids' to the roof; others are for cleansing the churchyard, probably from the mess left by the sheep always grazing there; also for constant clearing of nettles.

At the Easter Vestry in 1731 this resolution was passed, 'It is ordered . . . for the Future no money be given by the Church-wardens to any person or persons whatsoever who shall come with pass or passes or Certificates on any account or any pretence whatsoever'. The reason for this decision lies in the number of payments made to various travellers during the previous year or two, and to homeless, workless people. For instance, in 1730 twelve men begging for work and four disbanded soldiers received 11s. each; and between 1715–30 no less than 26 sailors. In 1723 there were many payments to 'travelling peapel . . . as do appear by a leetel boock the particulars'. About this time too a large number of men arrived in England from Turkey, owing to its disrupted state. Five had been in captivity and four who had worked there received 1s. each. Two men ruined by an inundation were also helped just before the Vestry refused all further aid. Of special interest are the entries for musical instruments used in the gallery at church services. In 1807 a new 'Claranett' cost £2 12s. 6d. Six years later £2 13s. 0d. was paid for another 'Clarinette and reeds'. New 'Bass' were bought from John Bridgeman and Mr Hill at £3 15s. 0d, and new strings most years cost 12s. Also from Bridgman, a Bell-founder, came a Bassoon 'for the use of the Parish': here is a pleasant fore-taste of Aldbourne's famous Silver Band. The purchase of a 'base vile' is also mentioned. These entries bring vividly to mind scenes in *Under the Greenwood Tree*. Then there was lighting for choir practice; candles cost £1 over a period of six years. Evening services were evidently not practicable in those days, otherwise far more candles would have been needed. Another set of entries centres round public events. On George IV's Coronation Day, 1s. 5d. was spent on 'Gunpowder for a charge on the Green', while a special Form of Prayer for 'the safe delivery of the Queen and birth of a Prince' cost 2s. There are payments for tolling the bell for the deaths of poor little Princess Charlotte, for the Queen in 1819 and George III in 1820. A curious discrepancy in labour costs is shown in the way that a man digging the graves received only 2s., but the sexton had 2s. 6d. for 'Cleansing ye Plate'. Other revealing entries, in 1694 are, '3 books of ffoxes Matrydons', 'one woolen and one linen cloth, for the communion table', 'a great bible', and '16 backets'—probably buckets in case of fire.

When agriculture was at an especially low ebb, the Church-wardens spent ninepence on postage for a pamphlet recommending the cultivation of potatoes, then less widely grown than turnips. Many are the payments for destruction of vermin. Thirty-nine polecats, almost certainly from the Chase, earned fourpence each between 1731–32; others are included under a general heading of 'varmints', also foxes and sparrows. One cannot help smiling at the way in which the Churchwardens, nearly all farmers, compensated themselves for the destruction of the latter at public expense. No less than 136 dozen were paid for in 1727 and in 1731, 253 dozen. Between 1783–1815 seventeen pounds went into their pockets. The farmer at the Warren did specially well for himself with payments amounting to £3 18s. 11½d. during two years. So also did Richard Church at Hillwood. In addition, farmers received money for 'corn to bait the sparrows'. The poor little hedgehog was persecuted then, as now: 50 'haghogs or hedgghoggs' were killed in one year, and 34 in another, at fourpence each. But foxes, at 1s. apiece, escaped lightly; many of the Churchwardens certainly hunted, and would have looked unfavourably on their destruction. Seven were paid for in 1732, and a few are included in general lists of vermin, but they drop out altogether after 1781, when hunting interests had grown too strong.

We may smile over the Churchwardens and their sparrows, but when one remembers all the unpaid work they did year after year, often sitting in a cold vestry at the end of a hard day, it would be unfair to grudge them these halfpennies.

SOME FORMER VICARS

The earliest recorded Vicar of Aldbourne is Richard de Whityng-digh; now Whittonditch, a small hamlet on the borders of Ramsbury and Aldbourne. The old thatched cottage beside the road was once a forge, worked by a real *black* Smith who enlivened Aldbourne Feast with his tricks in the early part of this century. The name has a special interest today because it has been given to the new group of parishes in this neighbourhood.

Little is known of the eight succeeding Vicars. The second, John Croke, may have been the Carmelite Friar recorded in Foster's Ecclesiastical Index. His date, as an Aldbourne Vicar, is 1396, but clearly there must have been another between him and Whityngdigh.

The first Vicar really to arouse interest is John Stone, appointed in 1478. On 1 December 1524 he bequeathed to 'the church of

St Mighel the suit of green velvet I bought late in London and to Jn. Jatt', to whom he also gave the lease of a house and land near Preston, a couple of miles away, on condition 'he shall find a light of 3 tapers to burn before St Mighel'. The church possesses no St Michael now, nor do we know what happened to him. It seems likely he disappeared with the Reformation. The velvet suit, the house, the visit to London prove Stone a man of substance, just as the request for tapers and the tomb inscription indicate his religious dedication. The Will remained unproved for 23 years after his death in 1501.

His successor, Dr John Edmunds, was also noteworthy in that he was appointed by Henry VIII because of his scholarly reputation, as one of the Cambridge conclave whose task it was to draw up 'prepositions of advice' on the intended divorce of Queen Catherine. To this he concurred, whether willingly or unwillingly we don't know. The next outstanding Vicar is John Lynche (1619), scholar of Jesus College Cambridge, and nominated by the Dean and Chapter of St Paul's. Simultaneously with his appointment as Vicar of Aldbourne he became a chaplain to the Bishop of Salisbury and Prebendary of the Cathedral. Perhaps his father-in-law John Chilmer, Bishop of London, helped his career: he stayed at Aldbourne for ten years. That he was an eloquent preacher and retained his standing with the Dean and Chapter of St Paul's, appears in their choice of him to preach at St Paul's Cross in Easter Week, 1637, on 'The Christian Passover'.

But his successor in 1630, Richard Steward, was a much more controversial and famous man. His history is arresting not only because of his close relationship with the Royal Family, but because, almost beyond doubt, it was he who took away the first Parish Registers. The Dictionary of National Biography tells us a lot about him. Three years after he became Vicar of Aldbourne Charles I appointed him one of his Chaplains and Clerk to the Closet, and later chose him to defend episcopacy at a meeting of the Church Commissioners in 1645. Here he 'spoke very learnedly (though seeming) forwardly against the Presbyterian movement'. The times were dark with foreboding, especially for an uncompromising Anglican like himself. When the Star Chamber convicted Prynne, Bastwick and Burton of sedition, and according to its brutal methods, ordered their ears to be cut off, a vast crowd of sympathisers, not surprisingly whatever their religious convictions, surrounded them during their ordeal. They cast, as C. V. Wedgwood tells us in *The King's Peace*, rosemary and sweet herbs at their feet, bringing them cups of water, dipping handkerchiefs in their blood. Archbishop Lang was deeply disturbed by the general turn of events, and so must Steward have been. Before he gave up Aldbourne in 1637 to be Provost of Eton he evidently thought anxiously about the Registers, especially when he considered the strength of the Puritan movement in Wiltshire. So he decided to ensure their safety till better times came. In 1646 the King entrusted him with the care of the Prince of Wales, and desired his son 'to defer to his opinions'. Henceforth he was constantly in the Prince's company, and must have included the Registers in his baggage when they escaped together via Scilly and Jersey to France, in 1650. The Aldbourne register starting from 1637 states that the earlier ones went to St Omer. Now St Omer, a Norman town that had somehow remained in English hands, possessed an English Catholic College (today a seminary). It would have been there that Steward left them, probably to perish when the town went back to France, or during the Revolution. All inquiries as to their present whereabouts have failed. So much for the Registers; now back to Steward himself. He was educated at Westminster School and Magdalen Hall, Oxford, where he distinguished himself, according to Antony Wood, as 'a good orator and eloquent preacher'. But whether he often stood in the pulpit of St Michael's Church seems doubtful since he was not only chaplain to the King, but also held two other livings, in the fashion of the time. England under Cromwell was no place for him. He spent his last two years in Paris and often preached there; very eloquent sermons, said John Evelyn, who went on to declare his death in 1651 as a 'great loss to the whole Church'. Clarendon described him as 'a very honest and learned gentleman whose heart was set upon the vindicating of the dignity and honour of the Church'. His body lies in the English Cemetery at St Germain des Pres. Eton owns his portrait. He holds a ribbon with a little golden angel hanging from it, sign that he was one of those who touched for 'The King's Evil'. Altogether he was a Vicar in whom Aldbourne may feel some pride, but also some regret for mistaken judgement.

How justified Richard Steward might have felt in his anxiety about the Registers is shown by what happened soon after his departure. In that same year, the Bishop of Salisbury, John Davenant, watched with dismay the unrest and disunity undermining the Church. In many places, including Aldbourne, the altar had been moved down into the body of the church and was treated with gross irreverence: there are instances of young men sitting on it, of children playing on it, and of a dog seizing a loaf of bread from it so that there was none left for the Sacrament.

The Bishop, a quiet, peace-loving man who took small part in politics, and probably dissociated himself from Laud's extremism, issued an order to the Curate (a term not used in our sense, but meaning someone entrusted with the care of souls) and Church-wardens of Aldbourne that the altar should be returned to its proper place, and 'that in order that the minister may neither be overtoyled nor the people indecentlie or inconvenientlie thronged at thrice in the year at least there be publicke notice in the church for four communions to be held upon four Sundies together; and that there come not to the Church above 100 at the most and the curate shall divide the parishioners into four parties according to his discretion . . . and if any turbulent spirit shall disobey this order he shall be proceeded against'.

It was an order not easy to carry out at such a period, for clearly the Communion Service had become a riotous occasion.

In 1782, the Curate, James Neale, had to answer a searching questionnaire from his Bishop, Skate Burrington, about his services. Neale reported Mattins every Sunday with a sermon, and another service, again with sermon, especially intended for servants, at 3 p.m.

In 1833, the Vicar, John Seagram, celebrated Communion, attended by 80 to 100 once a month; an increase from only 30 in previous years. Another Vicar, G. P. Cheather, worked valiantly for the restoration of the Church in 1867. One more Vicar, belonging to the present century, shall be included, namely W. H. Butler, a man of tremendous humanity and warm humour, who first served as curate here. A ten-year-old boy used to push heavy sacks of corn or meal in a barrow along a difficult, stony path, after he left school. Suddenly one day he was startled by a voice roaring, 'Stop'. Before he knew what was happening he found himself grasped in a strong pair of arms and dumped on top of his load. It was the new curate, who pushed him and his load for the rest of the way.

Butler was a universally loved man, of whom many still like to talk.

Altogether, as far as I can discover, Aldbourne has had 38 Vicars up to date, but as already noted there must have been at least one not recorded. Many were scholarly and devoted men with special gifts: Aldbourne has clearly always been considered an important living.

SIX

Hard Times and the Enclosure Act

PLAGUE

PROBABLY because of its isolated position, Aldbourne suffered less than many other towns and villages from the Plague. Marlborough had several severe outbreaks, due, it was believed, to visits from strolling players. However, the number of deaths in the village certainly rose in 1665 and 1666 from an average of 18 to 26, and this probably did not tell the whole story, since when the epidemic was at its worst, hasty burials in communal graves remained unrecorded. At any rate, Aldbourne received a grant in aid of stricken families in 1665.

FIRES

In the late summer of 1760 a terrible fire devastated the village, destroying not only many houses, but also barns full of corn, fustian, and material ready for weaving, to the value of £20,000. No one familiar with old folk-lore will be surprised to hear that for a long while afterwards a hare was said to have sat on a doorstep on the Green. Though the actual cause is unknown it may well be that a spark flew up from a fire in Bell Court.

Scarcely had the village recovered than another even worse fire followed. Richard Jefferies, drawing on old village records, described it graphically in the *Swindon Times*. Just as a farmer sat down to dinner news came that one of his ricks was smouldering. Quite unperturbed, he said, 'Wait till I've had my dinner. That'll be time enough . . .' But a few minutes later a labourer shouted through the window, 'Master, your rick is afire!' A strong westward wind drove the flames from one end of the village to the other, catching first a thatched barn and cottages in West Street, then spreading to the Green. It was August; the Pond at its lowest, and water for the two fire-engines hard to come by. As well as many houses, mostly thatched, 26 barns and much farm machinery were destroyed, and a number of sufferers crowded into the church that night for shelter. The village remained in a sad state for many months, and the next year Robert Wells sent a desperate appeal for help to the inhabitants of Reading, Hungerford, Lambourn, Wantage and Abingdon, because not nearly enough money had been collected locally. 'Let us therefore, fellow Christians, neighbours, and Countrymen', he writes, 'throw ourselves at your Feet and humbly beg your Aid.' How much help resulted we don't know, but the havoc had been great and the fustian trade permanently crippled.

Since the Overseers met soon after the fire to order the 'Chimney Peepers' to be diligent in their duties, it seems likely that this time a spark fell on a thatched roof. They declared that the two engines, nick-named Adam and Eve (now housed in the church, but in those days in a little building close below it), must be cleaned and repaired. These engines were often needed for smaller fires, as when one broke out in Baydon Street in 1793; the Churchwardens record paying the firemen 6s. for beer afterwards at the Blue Boar.

In May 1817 yet a fourth fire destroyed 15 cottages, three barns, two malthouses, the carpenter's and smith's shops, and much corn.

Again in 1914 Adam and Eve—now extremely old—came into action, when a woman in Castle Street lit her copper with a mass of paper under a faulty chimney. And a little later the King's Barn at Hightown went up in flames, together with the racing stables close by. The horses were rushed out but kept trying to return, and a pig in its sty at the Blue Boar was roasted to death.

After a long, hard life Adam and Eve, like two old-age pensioners, went into honourable retirement in 1924. They were replaced by a secondhand engine costing £40.

DISTRESS AND REVOLT

When the village had slowly recovered from these two big fires, another kind began to light up the skies. Wiltshire farm labourers, made desperate by acute poverty, with a wage of only seven shillings a week—the lowest anywhere in England—started burning ricks, breaking up what seemed to them their deadly enemy, farm machinery, and holding noisy demonstrations. The reason for the first recorded instance in Aldbourne is unknown. It probably sprang from some personal grievance combined with a general discontent. Late one evening in 1789 Adye Ayres, fustian manufacturer and constable, was disturbed by 'a great huzzaying and noise', so alarming that his wife fled out by the back door. When Adye ordered the crowd to disperse in the King's name, they only shouted insults, and John Cor, a member of the respected bell-founder family, said, 'They would not be gone but would come again every night and do what they had a mind to'. When Adye fetched a copy of the Proclamation declaring such assemblies illegal, they merely beat it from his hand, and continued to jeer; Cor even assaulted him. Adye reported all this to the authorities and preferred 'a bill of indictment' against the 'disturbers of his Peace and breakers of his window'. All this is reported in the Quarter

Session Rolls, but we are not told what happened to Cor and his company.

Within a few years far more serious troubles spread everywhere. Enclosure was well under way, though not in Aldbourne till early in the nineteenth century. But here as elsewhere there must certainly have been much hardship. The villagers, long accustomed to rabbitting on the Chase, suffered from the tightening up of the Game Laws in 1770. Between 1827–31, when poverty was perhaps at its worst, one in seven of every criminal conviction was for poaching, and over 8,000 men from all parts of England were sentenced, some for life transportation, others for seven years.

When, in 1800, an Act of Parliament recommended a Workhouse, the preamble began, 'Whereas the Parish of Aldbourne . . . is large and populous [just on 1,500 at that time] and the poor exceeding numerous', and continues that with a Workhouse, they 'might be kept employed and power given to compel them to work'. By this the designation 'pauper' is noticeably more frequent in the Parish Registers. The preamble accuses the three contemporary Overseers of misusing their office, so that the poor rate had increased to the great grievance of the landowners, and recommended the appointment 'of a fit and proper person' as an additional Overseer.

Here seems the moment for a little light relief in the midst of all this gloom. Among the Inkpen papers is an anonymous letter to 'the worship justics as sits at the bel at Ramsbury'. It is written on a large double sheet of very old paper, and on the back are the words, 'If the gustic not ther you may cart to layer rusels (lawyer Russells) for hele be zur to zee it'. The letter begins 'I am going to truble yur worsips with a view lines to let you know as ther is a fresh adismal overseer in the paris of aburn wer thers a ax of parment to chose won . . . he must be a person not conexted with any sort of bisness'. The writer goes on to suggest that the man likely to be chosen is the wrong one, and that it should be 'Varmer Warman . . . as had ben usd to it and ben overzeer many times bevore . . . and wud have don wel as any man in the paris . . . a gude naturd felow' . . . I must beg your worsips pardone for given you so much troble and must conclde your worsps most humble sarvent anown.' (Warman was a yeoman farmer and also an overseer). The writer adds a postscript, 'The auld man [Warman] woud luf to ze this but no won shall tel I get it safe in the box then I wil loke up at his window and zay gode nite and then get over the hill agen as vast as my legs will car me'.

The writer is a Ramsbury man, and he assures their worships he has no interest in the matter but that he 'lika vair play'. The letter, a long one, would delight Wiltshiremen, and apart from its fascinating spelling, it throws interesting light on this choice of an additional overseer, and of the manoeuvring that went on to prevent 'Varmer

Warman' from being the chosen man. He was an Aldbourne yeoman who also kept a shop and was suspected by the landowners of over-kindness to the poor. A London Trade Directory for 1792 includes his name, which helps to date this letter. No such accusation could be brought against the majority of overseers, whose predominant anxiety was to see that no rate-payers had to fork out money for either workless or rovers. But Wiltshire men at least showed compassion: the story is told in a copy of the *Devizes Gazette* for 1830. A starving old labourer, resting for a while by the roadside of a village further west, was driven out by a 'rout beggar' employed by the Overseers. He sank to the ground but the rout-beggar followed and dumped him on a passing coal cart; chucked out at the next village, he lay there exhausted and starving. Here, however, the Overseer had a heart, took him to his own house, sat him down by the fire and tried to get him to eat. But the poor old man was past all human help, and died soon afterwards.

The passing of the Enclosure Act for Aldbourne in 1805 brought sadness and a sense of loss. But apart from Enclosure, hardship intensified as a result of the French Wars, the Corn Laws, the Agricultural Revolution, the miserable wages. An early manifestation of growing discontent was a strike by housewives in various places, including Hungerford, over the high price of food. Desperate women seized supplies from shops, from carts, from a barge on the Canal, and sold them at what they thought a fair price.

In November 1830 far worse trouble broke out, first in Kent, then spreading to all parts of the country including Wiltshire. Agriculture was at a low ebb: tenant farmers found it difficult to meet their rents and tithes, and farm labourers to satisfy even their barest needs. Usually the riots were spontaneous, but were sometimes fanned by outside instigators. An 'Address to the Labourers of Wilts', began, 'Fellow Countrymen, beware of False Prophets. Beware of those who excite you to Riot and Tumult under pretence of improving your lot. Will the destruction of Cows give you Bread? . . . Where you have distress, rest assured that the Farmers and Landowners will do all in their Power to aleviate them. But the strong Hand of the Law *must* and *will* put down all Illegal Proceedings'. As indeed it did.

An example of a likely instigator, only a few miles from Aldbourne, is reported in the *Wiltshire Gazette*. On 25 November 1830 'a person mounted on a remarkably fine, dark, bay mare rode into Alton Barnes about 2 o'clock. . . . and after riding round the wheat rick proceeded at a moderate pace to Devizes. Mr Hitchcock at the moment was driving . . . through his farmyard, and his suspicions, being excited, he hailed the stranger . . . upon which he evidently alarmed put his horse into a gallop and actually took a desperate leap over a hedge and ditch . . . Mr Hitchcock completely lost sight of him'. 'A strict look-out for all visitors must be kept', the report continues, 'for their object might well be to cause destruction of ricks by throwing "combustible balls" into them'. Early the very day before this happened a riot broke out in Aldbourne. Mobs from both Ramsbury and Aldbourne had already been rioting and burning, but now matters reached a climax.

Broome Witts in his diary for 22 November 1830 describes how a mob, 400 or more . . . 'came here in the morning, broke threshing machines, and demanded a sovereign each, and money, beer, victuals from shops and houses.' They also broke windows and doors. Important people in Marlborough grew uneasy; they called a meeting at the Town Hall, and agreed that 'a band of respectable inhabitants enforced by cavarly' should either walk or ride to Aldbourne the very next day. So at 7 a.m. in the dim winter light, away they went, a company of 200 over the rough downland track, headed by a worthy clergyman, also by Mr Baskerville, of Rockley, who had recently been thrown off his horse by rioters, and other prominent landowners and magistrates. Arrived in Aldbourne, they found a crowd assembled. Twelve of 'the most desperate characters' were arrested, one of whom, probably after too much drink, 'had vowed he would have blood for his supper that night'. Then the Marlborough band proceeded to Ramsbury where they took 20 more. The ringleader here, a carrier and tanner, had waved a tricolour through the street the day before; proof of how strong was the influence still of the French Revolution. 'Today', gloats the reporter, 'he is the most abject being alive . . . he eluded his pursuers for a long time . . . at last he was discovered under a heap of leather and dragged from his hiding place'. The report declares, 'The peasantry generally have received the kindest treatment from the Farmers and it must have been some of the most desperate characters to induce them to act in the manner they have'.

In the same issue of the *Gazette* appears an appeal to 'All Persons willing to take upon themselves the Duty of Special Constables for the preservation of peace are requested to apply immediately to the Town Clerk', and a reward of £500 was offered to 'anyone giving information of damage to property or demanding money, provided this leads to conviction of the offender'. 'The King's gracious pardon' would be given to the informant if he himself were involved, but was not an actual perpetrator.

If the farmers, some of them perhaps, had given their men 'the kindest treatment' the same cannot be said of that meted out at Salisbury Assizes early in January 1831, when 34 Wiltshire and Dorset men were sentenced to death, 33 to life transportation, and others for 17 and 14 years. The *Salisbury Gazette* gives a full report of the trial. From Aldbourne 'a farmer named Goddard', a highly respected man, received seven years although he protested he had only gone with the mob to try to restrain them from violence. But one of the hostile witnesses, a landlord and Justice of the Peace, declared that Goddard had said that no farmer's word could be trusted, nor any gentleman except one, King William himself. A member of the old Aldbourne family of Pizzie also was given seven years' transportation. The trial makes heart-rending reading. One man, sentenced to death for leading a mob, 'appeared greatly moved and was in tears'. Still sadder was the case of a fourteen-year old boy, sentenced to life transportation, who, when removed from the dock, 'appeared greatly affected'; it is only fair to add that this terrible sentence was subsequently revised. W. H. Hudson in his *Shepherd's Life*, gives a moving, eye-witness's account of what happened at the end of the trial, as related to him by a woman of ninety-five, whose whole life had been passed at a village within sound of the Cathedral bells. She told how an anxious, weeping crowd of women gathered outside the Court Gates to learn their menfolks' fate. The men bravely did their best to cheer up their wives and mothers with cries of "'Tis hanging for me, but maybe there'll be a recommendation for mercy, so don't 'ee fret'; and another, 'Don't you cry, old girl, 'tis only fourteen years I've got, it may be I'll live to see you all again.' But many never returned, Aldbourne men among them.*

THE ENCLOSURE ACT

Enclosure of common lands went on for some 200 years before it reached Aldbourne. Leave to read its own Enclosure Act was given on 18 February 1805, and the final reading on 3 July. The preamble, like so many others, emphasises how the land was 'so circumstanced as to render the cultivation and manner thereof . . . incapable of any further improvement', and proceeds to point out how great were the advantages to all concerned of enclosure. Of course the promoters were right where larger landowners were concerned; but not so with humbler people, who, in a great many cases, suffered grievous hardship. One of the Commissioners himself, lamenting later the part he had played, said, 'The poor . . . may say with truth, "Parliament may be tender with Property. All I know is I had a cow and the Act has taken it from me"'. Thus reports Arthur Young, himself a strong advocate of Enclosure. Elsewhere he declares, 'The advantages of enclosing are now so well understood by all but a few old women who dislike it for no other reason but a love of singularity and a hatred of novelty'.

---

*Aldbourne relied on an unpaid, untrained Parish Constable for law and order, and because of his frequent inefficiency and helplessness, when an emergency arose, it was one of a few places in Wiltshire where, between 1832–36, a private association for the prosecution of felons was appointed. (Victoria County History, V. 243). This probably resulted from the riots in 1830.

It is true that in Aldbourne the results bore less hardly than in many places. Much land was already in the hands of the bigger farmers, but all the same a number of small-holdings in the four big Common Fields were lost, and though the owners received allotments in replacement they could no longer pasture a cow or a few sheep. This applied particularly to those now cut off from their bits of grazing ground on the downs. And apart from the difficulty of driving their sheep so far, they had also lost their supply of dung. One man, owning a cottage and garden in Windmill Field, bordering the Axford road, had to accept a much smaller piece of land down in the village. An elderly woman remembers the sense of bitterness that her father inherited from his father, over some deprivation he had suffered. And this must have been fairly general. So it is doubtful whether the majority of Aldbourne people felt in as festive mood as the Commissioners, when the Act was finally passed. This was the Bill of Fare presented to them by Thomas Odder (Alder?) at the Crown Inn at the end of their labours:

'*For the Comisherners* Chim (chine). Salt biff. Nats Tongue (Ox tongue). Half a lion of val byld. A neck of pork. Plenty of Balkin. A pair of ducks boyld', and, for vegetables, 'Collyflour Blockles. Spineg. Tornep Tops. Sprouts. Tates. Wattcress. Parsnops. Trnops. and a plenty of all sorts'; which certainly included plenty of drink. Some must have watched these well-fed men coming out of the Crown with hostile, brooding eyes. Apart from its consequences for the village, the text of the Act tells much of interest, such as the fact that the Malthouse on the Hungerford road was active then: that the Crown, the Bell, and the Blue Boar were all in being; that five weaving-shops existed; that Glebe Farmhouse was the Old Vicarage; that the little house at the north-west corner of the Green was still known as 'The Chantrey House'. Also it records the right of cottagers living up at Laines 'at all times to fetch water for their use until John Elderton (the Vicar) or his heirs make a good and sufficient pond, nearer to them than the existing one'. This they eventually did, but like so many little ponds, it is there no longer. The award was placed in the Church Chest, but after a while this caused friction, for the Vicar maintained his right to the key, and the Parish Council to theirs. So in the end they had a copy made to keep themselves, and sent the original Award to the County Record Office. It is a beautiful bit of work, rewarding to look at now, though less rewarding for some people at that time.

SEVEN

The Village in the mid-nineteenth century

THE Census for 1851 reveals most helpfully the composition of
the village at that date, when the population reached its peak for the
century, namely 1602. Naturally agricultural labourers and their
families formed a large majority, and the names of 362 appear,
including 15 Carters, 10 Ploughmen and boys, 17 Shepherds, and
1 Oxman. Some dozen or so were married women working with
their husbands. Seventeen farmers shared the labourers in differing
proportions. For example, William Brown at the Warren, with
1615 acres, employed 48 men, while Richard Church, at Dudmore,
could afford 23 men for his 630 acres. He also kept a gardener, a
groom, a charwoman, a servant, and a nurse. The same was true
of his sister-in-law, Ann Church, a widow, farming at Upper
Upham, though with rather fewer labourers per acre. Again,
Joseph Thorne at Snap, with 412 acres, had 15 labourers, two
shepherds, two carters, a ploughman and a groom. In contrast his
neighbour, Farmer Giles of Woodsend, kept only two men and a
shepherd for his 150 acres. Up at Stock Lane Thomas Kemm,
another well-to-do man, employed 18 labourers for his 500 acres.
At his house lived the shepherd, two carters, one labourer, a ploughboy, a servant and his groom. Broome Witts, once fustian manufacturer, farming 385 acres, kept 21 labourers, whereas at Laines
Farm, 250 acres, Thomas Butler managed with three men and a
ploughboy.

That there were 17 shepherds shown in the Census proves what
large flocks grazed the downs at that date; and that there were
four blacksmiths, one employing two adult sons, reveals the enormous importance of the horse. Shoeing was naturally their main
occupation, when all vehicles, ploughs and farm-machinery was
horse-drawn, and when every man who could afford it rode—anything from a fine hunter down to a small rough pony.

During the second half of the nineteenth century good blacksmiths started as apprentices, apparently in Hungerford, and a
certificate of competence in shoeing was awarded to those who
qualified. The daughter of one of Aldbourne's noteworthy smiths

possesses her father's award, a handsome, affair, so unlike the dull documents granted today. Shoeing involved not only hard work at the forge, but also long journeys in the early mornings, in order that the horses could get straight to work afterwards, and often they were in such a filthy state that the smith felt revolted by the stench. The time spent on mechanical repairs was small compared to that of shoeing. Still, there were ploughs, harrows, threshing-machines and so on to be kept in order. It is even possible that already the new-fangled Portable Engine was puffing away in Aldbourne, one placed at either end of the field, between them drawing the plough from one side to the other. Over 4,000 were at work in England by 1852, and the record of an engine-driver in the Census strengthens this possibility.

Then there was the harness. Four men helped to provide it; a saddlemaker, a harness-maker, and ostler, and a collar-maker for the large leather collars worn by the cart-horses. And people must be shod as well as horses. The number of shoemakers shows how much countrymen depended then on their local workmen: three shoemakers, four cordwainers, and one shoebinder, are listed. The cordwainers, who took their title from Cordova, once famous for its fine leather, may by that date have concentrated on a lighter kind of shoe for women, and for men not working out-of-doors. In the list of occupations revealed in the Baptismal Registers for the previous 16 years, the title 'Shoemaker' never appears; only that of 'Cordwainer', which looks as if the old title was still in general use, and that no differentiation existed.

No less than eight tailors supplied village needs, most of them probably kept busy over the stout, long-lasting fustian suits still worn by many of the men early in the nineteenth century. The actual fustian trade in the village was now almost dead; only one woman working with her two daughters, and another, an octogenarian, kept it just alive. But local shops continued to stock the cloth, and one must remember its immense durability. Four 'rag-gatherers'—two men and their wives—are likely to have included fustian in their pickings.

In 1867, according to Pigot's Commercial Directory, the number of tailors had dropped to two; and to only one, chiefly engaged on repairs, early in the twentieth century. Besides the tailors there were a shirt-maker, six dressmakers, and a bonnet-maker, using the famous willow plait, then at the height of its popularity. A hundred and one willow weavers, mostly women and children, are recorded. Five children made baskets, some of exquisite fineness. Six willow-cutters provided the wood for bonnets and hats, baskets, and for willow-squares for export to London. A whalebone cutter, named in an earlier record, and presumably turning out bones for women's stays, does not reappear.

Seven bakers supplied the village with bread and also baked the loaves brought to them, in their ovens. Most of the bakers sold groceries as well as bread; in addition there were two grocers' shops. The village had only one butcher: meat was still a luxury for the poorer inhabitants, and most of them kept their own pig, and their own poultry, and would have depended a lot on rabbits from the Chase. An itinerant meat-dealer is also recorded. Four other people appear as 'Shop-Keepers'. Two laundresses presumably washed for the wealthier class, and the same would be true of the 21 domestic servants and four charwomen.

Coming back to the men, we find eight woodmen and wood-cutters, but only one is specifically named as hurdle-maker, which seems strange considering the importance of the hurdle to sheep-farming. The likely explanation is that the men listed as wood-cutters were also making hurdles in the woods. A member of the notable Jerram family was a cooper; two maltsters were at work; a miller on Baydon Hill ground much of the corn, and four inns sold the local beer—the Queen, the Bell, the Crown and the Blue Boar. The two latter are still going strong. One coal dealer supplied the villagers with fuel, but also, at that date, living as they did in a well-wooded neighbourhood, they would then have warmed themselves and heated coppers and ovens with logs and wood-chips.

Building is represented by three masons, one brickmaker, employing two men, two bricklayers, one painter, and two journeymen. No doctor is recorded; when needed, one probably came from Marlborough or Hungerford, But there were two midwives, and a traveller in drugs was staying in the village at the time of the Census.

The names of four schoolmasters or mistresses, and of over 100 scholars, indicates what strides education was making, even though a real village school was not built by the National Society till 1857. Though the Baptismal Registers for 1841 bear witness to a Police Constable, he had disappeared ten years later.

Altogether the Census suggests that Aldbourne was a flourishing, self-supporting village in the mid-nineteenth century.

EIGHT

Old Names and Old Inhabitants

ALL villages possess intriguing lists of good country names; certainly Aldbourne does, its own starting as 'Ealinchurnam'.

In old deeds and records occur titles of such flavour as Budge Bush, Cousinage Corner, Cathangers, Hobbs' Hill, Mushes, and White Shard (these two still so called), Hay Lynch, Penticoots (now Penticote, once probably Penticost), Bestroppa, Cow Crout Barn, Upham Moonlight, World's End (now Woodsend), White-shard and Rooks Wood. Beside this wood once stood a house bequeathed by Roger Walrond to his daughter in 1611, with the provision that she 'make sufficient estate'. Moonlight, an upland field, is a name still familiar to some old people and probably dates back to poaching days.

Aldbourne surnames, too, cast their spell: Vockings, a very early one, may derive from 'Vikings'; Bacon is another early one. Bits of land in the East and West Common Fields were called after this family, and so was an eight-acre field. The first Bacon married Anne, in 1637, and other Bacons continued for 156 years. I always hoped to find one of the equally numerous Salts marrying a Bacon, but never did, though both had babies christened on the same day. Thomas Bacon kept the first village Post Office.

Other suggestive names are Rye and Barley. In 1601 Stephen Barley left his 'horse, beestes and sheep', to his two sons, and desired 'to be buried within the church of Auburne'. Then there are the Knackstones. John Knackstone indicted William Fowler for singing a libellous song about him in 1629, but though he read it out at the Quarter Sessions he lost his case. In 1734 a Knackstone, himself a Constable, is presented at the Manor Court 'for feeding his horses on the waste'.

Hedges, Hawthornes, Elderfield, Alder, Hazel, Birch, Ivy and Woodruff are true country names. A Woodruff once kept the inn. The name is redolent of the little white flower that beautifies our copses, once treasured by housewives for scenting their linen-chests. Then there are Applefield and Orchard; Orchards were well-known as chairmakers, and previously as thatchers and woodmen. Eatwell seems appropriate for a time when food was still plentiful, For birds, we find Finch and Sparrow. A Sparrow's will was proved in 1599; another was living here in 1646; a Finch still earlier. Other good names are Corduroy and Bigbow. Occupational names are frequent. Fowler has already been mentioned. A downland village naturally always had a Shepherd, originally spelt Sheepherd; innumerable Palmers recall pilgrims carrying their willow wands. They are still with us.

Naturally some surnames derive from places. 'Vize' crops up often from 1638 well on into the eighteenth century; Burford is another. Both link themselves with Aldbourne's big sales of sheep and wool. Devizes, formerly 'The Vize' held an important sheep market, and Burford was a flourishing wool town. Liddiard, in a variety of spellings, is a north Wiltshire place name, and has continued for over 300 years. Other evergreen families are Barnes, Barrett and Stacey. Jerrams, of Norman origin, have played a part for over 200 years.

Among old village families no longer here must be mentioned the Motts, important landowners in the eighteenth century. An assessment in 1795 includes pieces of land, called Motts, as well as Motley Croft. William was a Churchwarden, and administered Richard Goddard's Charity. The Churchwardens' Accounts for 1715 record, 'Received of Mr. Mott two pounds for ye youse of ye poor gave by Mr Goddard . . . due at Mikelmas'. Goddards and Walronds, both exalted and humble, inhabited the village from earliest days.

The Browns, to become Lords of the Manor in 1894, first appear in 1655, and continue in one of their numerous branches right on to the present day. Edward Coward, a noted Wiltshire farmer, writing of farming in the nineteenth century says, 'Of all farming families in the County the Browns were by far the most numerous and influential . . . There was a time when one could walk from Horton to Wantage, and scarce set foot on land not occupied by a Brown'. Brown, a solid country name, conjures up fustian, ploughed fields, the downs in winter, the dark trunks of elms.

The Adee family, important in the seventeenth century, held special interests in the Chase. John Adee issued his own trade token, valued at one farthing and bearing a picture of three rabbits, in 1656.

Turning from surnames to Christian ones, here are a few that people are not likely to choose again: Abigail, Arabella, Eunice, Triphena, Leah, Theophilus, Sharch, Gadislad, Zabulon (Absolom?), Zaccharias, Zephenia, Cornelius and Ephraim. Bible names were understandably popular in the mid-seventeenth century.

SOME OLD INHABITANTS

I start with four soldiers. Colonel Doyley, bearing one of the oldest village names, emigrated to Jamaica with other soldiers during the

Civil War. He organised them with such skill combined with severity that he was able to colonise the island for Britain, and he became its first Governor. He judged the constitution of his own country as suitable for Jamaica. On retirement he chose St Martin-in-the-Fields, instead of Aldbourne.

A second soldier, Robert Drewe, again of an old Aldbourne family, served in the 20th Foot, first in the Peninsular War, then at New Orleans after the American War of Independence, then back again to Europe and to peace on the island of St Helena where he helped to guard Napoleon. One wonders what he, a splendid-looking man 6 ft 2in. in height, thought as he watched that small frustrated figure pacing endlessly to and fro. When Napoleon died of cancer in 1821 Drewe was chosen, as one of the six tallest soldiers, to help carry the coffin. He himself enjoyed far more honourable retirement in his native village, where his tall old figure walking the countryside was a familiar sight. On one of his journeys to Hungerford to fetch his pension he sat down by the wayside and quietly died.

Now comes John Wakefield, of the old Wiltshire Regiment, who suffered even greater hardship in the scorching heat and privation of our sadly mistaken war in Afghanistan. When he too returned to Aldbourne he talked of the terrible march to relieve Kandahar; of the crossing of the mountains between India and Baluchistan with a battery drawn by elephants; of the way the enemy attacked suddenly from behind the rocks. Scarcely was this ordeal over than he was caught up in the First Boer War, where on Majuba Hill his regiment suffered most grievous losses.

But again an Aldbourne man showed the power to live an active life in spite of all he had previously endured, when he settled down in Lottage in a house which he named Kandahar. Not only did he often walk 16 miles a day as an auxiliary postman, but he gave physical instruction to the children and taught musketry to the young men. At his funeral in 1940 five soldiers carried his coffin and a bugler from his old regiment sounded the 'Last Post'.

Another Aldbourne man became British Army Instructor in Unarmed Combat, and he, with five other wrestlers of international repute, gave an exciting demonstration in the Village Hall.

The First World War produced worthy successors to Drewe and Wakefield. One, when a company of the Wiltshire Regiment was raked by fire from a machine gun, volunteered to silence it. When no bombs were available he found some left by the Germans, carried as many as he could round his neck, crawled to the gun, threw his bombs and destroyed it and its crew. A sniper caught sight of him, fired, and wounded him in the shoulder. He recovered and was awarded the D.C.M.

And now for one last military hero, or rather, heroine; Maud Hawkins, later known by her code-name of 'Pat'. She married a Frenchman, and during the Resistance Movement they harboured many escaping prisoners and also transmitted messages to London. But for this she paid a heavy price. She was captured by the Gestapo, sent to Ravensbruck Concentration Camp and set to road-making, on a diet of bread made of horse-chestnuts and cabbage-leaf soup. Her weight, a very moderate one, halved in a few weeks. Nor was this all. A guard smashed a broomstick over her head, and left her with a broken hand and impaired sight and hearing (later, an operation in Switzerland restored her). Just before the war ended, deemed useless now, Pat was transferred to an extermination camp. All hope seemed gone, but mercifully, miraculously, the Americans bombed the gas chambers just in time to save her. No wonder she received the French Legion of Honour and the *Croix de Guerre*; also the American Freedom and the British Empire medals. A portrait of her wearing her decorations won a Gold Medal at the Academie Royale in Paris. She is someone in whom Aldbourne may well feel pride.

Civilian inhabitants now come into the picture. Henry Martin (d. 1721) belonged to a family which lived at Snap. Though a lawyer, he was never well enough to attend the courts, so he took to writing for 'The Spectator', and because he contributed to the rejection of a treaty of commerce with France was rewarded with the post of Inspector General of Imports and Exports. Not a very inspiring person, nor closely knit with the village. Of those who were, none are more so than the Pizzies. The name is intriguing and people used to say that the family came from Italy. But although there were Italians name Pizzi in north Italy (one a sculptor), the name is entirely English and derives from Pusey in Berkshire. It crops up in several surrounding villages in a variety of spellings such as Pizey, Puzey, Peasy, Pezey, and Pizzey; a Pizey is recorded at Hedgerley in 1591. The earliest Pizzies were probably Phebe, buried in 1679, and another of the name who acted as Churchwarden in 1663. From then onwards there are few years during the next 200 when Pizzies are not being born, married, or buried. They followed a variety of callings. One was a shoemaker, one a maltster, two were shepherds, one, William, a prosperous pioneer of the willow trade who carried on his business in Hightown. His father, Joseph (Joseph and Joshua were favourite Pizzie names), helped to add a bell to St Michael's. William was a devoted ringer who taught the village boys the art, and himself took part in the Grandsire Triples that celebrated Queen Victoria's accession.

Pizzies, often well to-do, owned a bit of land called 'Pizzies'. Though some served as Churchwardens, others joined the Dissenters in the eighteenth century, but returned to the Anglican Church later. Caleb was baptised in 1818 aged sixty-five. Sadly at last the line died with two brothers, neither of whom left an heir. The elder was a shepherd at Manor Farm for many years; a little bent man, a lover of solitude, who found it both on the wide open downs and in his bungalow tucked snugly under them. When too old to tend the sheep he pushed the baby from the Manor about the village, and grew more sociable. One day, some Americans motoring past stopped for a better look at this old man with the perambulator. 'All straps, wrist-watches and cameras', as an onlooker described them, they sprang out crying, 'Hold it, mister, hold it!' Click went their cameras. Perhaps old Pizzie and that baby girl are still shown in the U.S.A. to illustrate the 'quaintness' of English village life.

His brother, Siddie, represents a different type; small but very upright, like a little ferret with sharp, bright, twinkling eyes. His skin grew walnut brown from weather and dirt. When someone visited him in hospital they were startled at sight of his *white* hands; hands always so dark before. Housework was not in his line, and his house was invariably filthy. Sometimes he would ask a neighbour in for a sip of port. Out came glasses thick with dust, but she never had the heart to refuse or to wipe her own first. When later he shared his home with another old man they each claimed their own half of the stairs. Siddie's side remained unswept; the other ostentatiously clean. He washed all his clothes once in six months, when the little yard became almost impenetrable. Siddie was a born poacher, and an adept at finding his way about in dark woodlands. Once, after working a while with two builders on a house near Savernake Forest he grew bored and set off to walk home alone on an autumn evening, grew tired and sat down under a tree. Word went out that he was missing, but an extensive search by the light of lanterns at last revealed him asleep, the leaves thick about him. Like a babe in the wood, they said.

Siddie was often seen feeding a child on either side with sticky sweets from his pocket. At Carnival time he always appeared in some wonderful guise. Last of the Aldbourne Pizzies, he undoubtedly added much to village gaiety; we don't breed many such people now.

It would be hard to find a family more unlike the Pizzies than the Goddards, originally 'God-hard', well established in the neighbourhood by the early sixteenth century as sheep farmers. In 1527 the Abbess of Lacock granted a lease of land at Upham to John Goddard, 'a woolman'. When the Monastery was dissolved Henry VIII gave John the land, and his son Thomas is believed to have rebuilt the old house. But the history of the Goddard family is too long, too complicated, to embark on here. It is enough to recall the tower that Richard helped to build, the bell inscribed with a prayer for his soul that still rings, the little footpath running between Lottage and Grazills; the imposing family monument in the church. The Walronds, another long-lasting family, have already come into the story.

The Staceys are a prolific race. I have spoken of the shop and the lively lady who kept it. Her husband was both baker and bandmaster, who himself played a variety of instruments and took the Band to many a contest in a horse-drawn coach. Late at night he returned, not to sleep but to bake bread. Another Stacey also kept a shop where, among other delicacies, she sold pigs' trotters. But the sight of boys eating them outside and then scattering the bones about made her furious, and she gave up the sale of trotters. Entertainments were often livened by her monologues in rich dialect. Those in the know could buy a jar of her 'White Oils', considered an infallible cure for rheumatism and made from her own secret recipe. Her universally-loved daughter, and later her grandson, succeeded her.

Then there are the Barnes. Billy Barnes, town-crier in the first half of this century, cried in a tailed coat with red binding and a tall beaver hat. He was a fine figure of a man, with a powerful voice, who came high in All England Town Crier competitions. For these he practised on top of the Southward, with a friend stationed on Greenhill, half a mile away, to listen. His voice came across clear as a bell. Once he was asked to broadcast because of his rich dialect. 'We all spoke it once', he said, 'till new folk came to the village with their brogues.'

When the Parish Council shirked the sending out of notices Billy cried them at 11 different places for 1s. a cry. Later when people refused to pay even enough for a drink of beer, he decided to retire. He is dead now but both his bell and his memory remain.

Two women nature-lovers enriched the village. Emily Sophia Todd (1859–1949), a devoted botanist, gradually built up a herbarium that contained specimens of nearly every English wild flower. Her collection went to Swindon Museum, but has sadly disintegrated. Two plants that she discovered were named after her; one a variety of the Wood-cowwheat (*Melampyrum sylvaticum*), another a wild rose, *Rosa Toddie*. Her broad figure, clad in a tweed suit, was a familiar sight as she cycled about, her back tyre always flat. When eighty years of age, she waded barefoot in a marsh to reach a rare plant, and hung over a cliff after another while her companion, as thin as she was stout, precariously held her ankles.

Muriel Foster, lover of all wildlife, especially birds, has already been spoken of. Among other well-remembered characters are five spinster sisters, noted for their charitable offerings of soups and jellies, and their Bible-readings to the sick and bedridden; also for their habit of walking in two pairs, while the fifth sister went her solitary way. But once they closed ranks: after a quarrel with the

Vicar, they tramped together seven miles over the downs to Ashbury every Sunday for many weeks.

Mrs Onion Jam lived in the cottage known as Lower Sixpenny. One year, overwhelmed by an enormous onion crop, she decided to use part of it for jam. 'But somehow,' she lamented, 'it doant zeem to taste right.' After that the title stuck, and her son, like herself a simple soul, was always called Billonions. Another example of the countryman's love of nick-names is found in that of 'Thunder and Lightning' given to a certain couple; she of a fiery nature, and he the one who growled back. Next door to Mrs Onion Jam lived Tommy Tucker. If he didn't actually sing for his supper, he could wax extremely merry after a drink at the inn.

Early this century the Mail was driven from Swindon to Hungerford in a covered cart drawn by two horses. After the driver had been held up in the dark on the lonely road over the downs he took to carrying a pepper-pot and talking to himself continuously. This, he reasoned, would warn dangerous characters that he was not alone. At Aldbourne he always tied up his horses and took a drink at the Queen before going on to Hungerford.

Of four men, one dead, three still alive, I will write a little more fully. Aldbourne has bred many people who have helped to sustain a fine countryside. One, whose name, Woolford, shows that his ancestors once warded off wolves from the sheep, for 50 years walked behind his plough, drove the wagons, and tended the horses. When the last was led away, in 1959, he accepted it philosophically, and with the dry humour so typical of his sort, he asked a neighbour,

'D'ye have a sausage for your breakfast?'

'On Sundays,' she replied.

'Then mebbe you'll be eating old Colonel before long,' said he. Yet he had been devoted to Colonel and to all his horses.

In retirement his garden brought him immense satisfaction; the sight of the first leaves of a 'spud', the first broad beans, made his day. And he liked to sit beside his door gazing proudly at a row of rigid, flaunting gladioli. But he had, too, an eye for his white violets, and for an amazing bush of Love-in-the-Mist that had sprung up under his window. Surprisingly, since he left school at ten, he was an avid reader. *Under the Greenwood Tree* and *Lark Rise to Candleford* were among his favourites, as was the Bible. The Salvation Army with its cheerful music and simple faith attracted him more than any other religious body. He was never one to think 'this world is very evil' or that life is a desert to be crossed before the Promised Land can be reached. He loved it almost till the end; ''Twould be a waste of time to die', he used to say.

Another man, a dairy farmer now retired, remembers how, when he left school at twelve, he worked ten hours a day for 3s. a week, and sometimes felt so hungry that he would share a turnip with the sheep. In early days he made hurdles in the woods, where he grew familiar with a great variety of birds. His keen eye missed nothing, whether it be a kestrel overhead, a brambling in the hedge, or some small object on the ground. Once, as he ploughed round the site of the old windmill, he picked up a horsebrass engraved with a windmill. Other finds include a wealth of coins, one struck in the last year of Charles I; trade tokens; flint arrowheads; fossils, including a perfect Shepherd's Crown; and a large, shining, cone-shaped shell.

One day his plough struck something hard. 'Stop!' he cried to his companion, 'there's summat here!' They ploughed deeper and up came a great thunderbolt, undoubtedly shed during a terrific storm a few days before. When harrowing he would detect strips of sickly yellow contrasting with the healthy green all round. 'Them young chaps scamping their work when they spread the muck', he would mutter.

His ear was quick as a bird's to catch any strange sound. Once, standing by his gate, watching water streaming along after a downpour, he heard the chink of metal. He put his hand down and drew up a Victorian Jubilee Medallion. With a herd of over 50 cows, he knew each by name. He served on the Parish Council for 50 years, and nobody was more familiar with all Rights of Way, or guarded them more zealously.

A second man still with us has also been a staunch Parish Councillor for even longer and chairman of it for 20 years, and has also served on both Rural and County Councils. He is a most deceptive person. His mild face, his slow, gentle voice when he took the chair at a difficult meeting would make newcomers think, 'Goodness! He'll never get through all this contentious business!' But calmly, patiently, firmly, he could always steer his way to the end. Other voices might be raised loudly, but it was the quiet one that prevailed. As a convinced Socialist—a true Christian Socialist—he met much hostility in the more intolerant past. Once, after he had raised his voice in protest at a Conservative meeting two indignant retired colonels threatened to withdraw their custom from his little shop for airing such dangerous views.

'That's your affair,' replied he. 'I don't try to sell my politics when I do business, but outside I have as much right as you to express my own opinions.' The colonels walked away muttering, but next morning their wives came to shop as usual.

My third still-living man, whose name shows him to be of Norman origin, has sung for 70 years in the choir of the church which he has helped to keep in repair ever since, as a boy, he stood on his father's shoulder to mend the leaded windows. Furthermore, he played in the Band for quite 50 years, was Bandmaster for a considerable time, and in the First World War was one of a number of fellow bandsmen to cheer the hearts of their comrades with their music amid the mud and misery of Flanders. After enduring much pain with fortitude he has just had a leg amputated.

We have an outstanding woman too; a fit survivor of the old Orchard family. Her parents kept the village post office for years, and she herself as a girl carried letters and telegrams by foot or on her cycle to the farthest bounds of the parish, including Snap, where grand old Rachel Fisher would refresh her with a cup of tea. She loves music and often sang as she went along. Later she and her husband also kept the post office. And no matter how busy she might be she has always found time both to lead and share in village activities.

Another stout-hearted woman reared 13 children in a small cottage. The eldest was grown up when the last was born, and she would carry it, strapped in a basket on her cycle, to fetch the daily papers from Hungerford and so eke out the small family income.

THE FEAST

These had been magic words for the village ever since the Church Council meeting at Oxford in 1222 ordained that all parishes should keep their own Saints' Days as secular as well as religious festivals. At that time Aldbourne Church was still dedicated to St Mary Magadalen (of lower status now in the Roman Calendar), which led to the Feast being fixed for the first Monday after 22 July, and it has so remained ever since. Probably from very early days a Fair has arrived in the village, but unlike many others, it actually possesses no Charter.

The word 'feast' is less magical perhaps now than when the villagers depended far more on their own resources for amusement. It was once a truly outstanding occasion, and old people talk nostalgically of what happened when they were young. Absent members of the family, former inhabitants and old friends, flocked back. Houses were redecorated, walls repapered with paper costing, in the early twentieth century, twopence a roll; brooms plied so vigorously that spiders were said to hold up traffic on the hill. 'Viggety' puddings, sometimes a yard long, tied in cloths, were boiled in the coppers or on the fire, together with a sheep's head, ham or bacon, and vegetables. One small boy, left to watch the cooking while his mother went to church, rushed to fetch her home. 'Please come quick!' he whispered, 'that old head be gobbling up the vegetables.'

The Fair people, still usually called gipsies in those days, were not allowed to enter the village till after 7 p.m. on Sunday evening. But long before that boys ran out beyond Lottage, or along South or West Streets to lay their heads on the ground and listen for the sound of approaching horses. If a caravan was reported from another direction away they rushed to escort it in to the village. Great activity followed as one after another arrived. Horses were led off to drink at the Pond before going to graze in a nearby meadow. Then, on the slopes below Beech Knoll, came the Camp meeting, a religious ceremony inaugurated by a Derbyshire Methodist couple, who had formerly lived in a hamlet called Mow Cop; they so named their new home on Baydon Hill. People from all round attended, and the singing was extremely hearty. One old lady who had been promised a new dress for the feast got so worked up that her repeated cries of 'Alleluia' and 'Praise the Lord', so disturbed the congregation that the speaker admonished her: 'Now you just be quiet or there'll be no new dress for you.'

Once, when the feast lasted two or three days, two speakers from Wanborough stayed with an old couple who had boiled a ham in their honour. Not one morsel remained when they departed. Always at daybreak next morning preparations were in full swing. The womenfolk made sweets at the back of their caravans in conditions that would have given a Food Inspector a fit today. A mother and two daughters from Buckland in the White Horse Vale, scrupulously clean and tidy in black dresses and white aprons in contrast to the gipsy women, also made sweets from a sticky mixture attached to the posts in front of the pond, and stretched out for yards before being cut up. Mussels, cockles, and winkles dressed with vinegar were on sale, as well as fried fish. A childrens' roundabout was either turned by hand, or by a pony, and a larger one by a small steam-engine. Other attractions included 'Phoebe', with a head and no body (a trick done by mirrors); the blacksmith from Whittonditch, who walked on upturned nails and put red-hot irons in his mouth; and, of course, fortune-telling. Because the village boys rushed about with water pistols, the girls wore clean print frocks but never their Sunday best; for years the Parish Council tried to stop this practice.

The outstanding, if rather bloody, sport was the backswording which persisted into the 1890s. Men fought each other with stout sticks on platforms of upturned beer barrels, till blood poured from their foreheads; and they queued up to wash themselves at the Pond. Two White Horse Vale champions paid half-a-crown to all who took them on, while a local Goliath acted as M.C. and himself fought any challenger. More promiscuous fighting began in the evening when beer, made from hops and malt in the village, flowed freely at only a penny a pint. Woe betide any foreigner who dared raise a scoffing cry of 'Dabchick' then: into the Pond he went.

Nowadays the feast is a tamer, and of course, far more highly mechanised, affair. The Travellers, no longer Gipsies, are wonderfully tidy, and their gaily painted caravans have been replaced by ones luxuriously fitted. Their apparatus is far more elaborate, but also far more predictable. Inevitably the character of the feast has changed. Everything is bigger, faster, noisier, more glittering. The old gentle roundabouts with their beautiful gilt horses have been replaced by machines that whisk you round at break-neck speed; swing-boats soar higher and higher; a terrifying machine called an Octopus attracts the young, as also do the Dodgems. Still, the feast reunites families and renews old friendships, and the church, floodlit and beautiful, looks down on a scene it has witnessed for more than 750 years.

NINE

The Village in later days

MANY things in the second half of the nineteenth and first half of the twentieth centuries changed, developed, and enriched village life.

RELIGION

A strong, widespread revival, sometimes genuinely religious, sometimes motivated by the desire of the well-to-do to keep the poor in their proper places, produced a multiplication of churches and chapels throughout England. The example set by the Wesleyans in 1840, in West Street, was followed in Lottage by the Methodists four years later, and by the Baptists, in Back Lane, in 1846. These were all due to a devoted band of men whose fathers, grandfathers, and great-grandfathers had fought for over 200 years to worship in their own way. They had mostly been poor men, unable to afford a building of their own, meeting together on Sundays in each other's houses. At last, with some slight improvement in economic conditions, and the continuing inspiration, long after his death, of John Wesley, they could express their belief in concrete form.

Their preachers included several outstanding characters. There was William Martin, known as 'Sunday School Martin', who daily walked from the Butts to Wanborough Plain Farm, and gave generously out of his small wage for the cause so dear to him, supplemented by the sale of old coins and flints picked up as he worked in the fields. Faithful to the last in his belief that in the Sunday School lay the best hope for the coming generation, he left £50 each to both Lottage and West Street schools.

Another was a club-footed man named Sherman who, when the appointed preacher failed to arrive, marched up the aisle, saying as he went, 'I wouldn't give tuppence for the soldier of Christ who didn't have his own armour buckled on to fight at a moment's notice'. A third, Silas Newman, a roadman, had a tremendous knowledge of the Bible and helped all willing to profit by it.

Every year the Methodists and Wesleyans combined in a midnight Watchnight service, and when it ended they went out and sang Isaac Watts' hymn 'Before Jehovah's awful throne' in different parts of the village. No ecumenical movement existed then and this practice must surely have irritated many. But the most widely attended and important of the outdoor Dissenter services was the one held on a hillside field at feast time. More of this later.

In 1857 a considerable restoration of St Michael's was carried out, but ten years later the need for further work grew urgent. The roof leaked; the arches were out of the perpendicular; the floor-boards were rotten; the old pews of 'irregular and unseemly height'; the galleries and the ringing-loft blocked the west window. A coat of whitewash hid the beauty of the stonework and the moulding of the arches. But, reported the *Marlborough Times*, 'The Venerable and esteemed Vicar and his parishioners found great difficulty in the accomplishment of the object on which they had set their hearts'. £2,000 was needed; a large sum for a not very rich village. But love for their church, once so beautiful, now in such a sorry state, inspired people to immense activity, led by the Vicar's wife. The Vicar, responding to a vote of thanks, told how his wife, when she had collected her first sixpence, 'pounced on every sixpence I could spare . . . no more comfits or lollypops for me'.

To the celebration service came the Bishop, the Archdeacon, and countless clergy. From the Vicarage up on the hill they went in procession to the church, singing Psalm 132. Afterwards the bells, rung now from the base of the tower, 'pealed out over the broad depth of down . . . giving loud utterance to the rejoicing that filled so many hearts below'. And to their music 200 guests ate 'a substantial luncheon of a most recherché character' in a marquee on the Green. Long speeches and many votes of thanks, followed. Edne Witts, of the famous fustian family, came in for special mention by both Bishop and Archdeacon. The Bishop thoughtfully begged his listeners to go on eating while he spoke. The left-overs were distributed among the poor and the children. One incident slightly marred the festivities. A stationary horse, harnessed to a cab, and very bored, got loose and bolted through the village, scattering the crowd. 'The horse, a vicious animal', said the report, 'kicked the driver off his seat, ran up a bank and turned the fly over, then fled into a field a mile away.'

EDUCATION

An event of paramount importance was the building of the first real village school in 1858, a typical neo-Gothic red-brick building designed by H. Butterfield. Whatever its artistic merits or demerits, it must have been warmly welcomed by many parents who longed for their children to be better educated than themselves. That they were numerous is proved by the 1851 Census, where close on 100 'scholars' are recorded, several from out-lying districts. These

depended on small, part-time schools, subsidised by local bene-
factors or by church and chapel, staffed by unqualified teachers in
their spare time. Such a one stood beside what was then a public
footpath named Bouchers Lane, running by Rose Cottage and on
past a cottage called, for no accountable reason, 'The Old Priest's
House'. The little school was built, like Rose Cottage, formerly
'Cor's', in the late fifteenth century, and a part of it still stands, dark,
damp and overgrown with ivy. Late in the nineteenth and early
twentieth century the teacher was a postman, who before he started
work in the school walked over 16 miles with letters for Upper
Upham and North Farm. For this long tramp, seven days a week,
he received a wage of seven shillings. Also, at what is now Brook
Cottage, another school, largely a night school, functioned. To it
came not only children, but also boys and girls with love letters
they wanted read or written for them.

That there were so many 'scholars' before any Education Act
came into being was perhaps partly due to the strong concern for
education in both Swindon and Marlborough. By 1905, 127 older
children were being taught in Aldbourne, mainly by a headmistress
at a salary of £45 a year, assisted by two monitresses at £7 10s. od.
The headmistress was a fragile-looking woman who, however, held
her own against certain rough, unruly boys when they kicked and
fought her, and by sheer weight of personality she could extract
the truth from any who lied to her. At times, when things got very
bad, she would send out a cry for help to one of the School managers.

In 1873 an Infant School was added, and by the beginning of the
century was attended by 103 small children, many surprisingly
young, only three or four years old. One man remembers going as a
tiny boy from Baydon Hill; walking home for dinner; returning
only to fall fast asleep with his companions, their long curls falling
over each others' shoulders.

This village school, a Church one, but for most of its life accepted
tolerantly by Dissenters, provided a sound education for some 100
years. However, despite the affection felt for it by a few old inhabitants, its drawbacks were many. It was dark, with high, narrow,
windows; hard to warm; often excessively damp. Small wonder that
all most deeply affected welcomed a new, well-designed building
in 1963.

OFF TO PATAGONIA

When agriculture reached a low ebb in the last quarter of the
nineteenth century, a member of the Walrond family decided to
emigrate from Ramsbury to Tierra del Fuego in Patagonia, and to
take a band of workers with him. Though the greater number
belonged to his own village, several Aldbourne men went too.

Since many had never even been outside their own county, their courage seems amazing. Suddenly their peaceful small-scale surroundings were replaced by a vast country, eternally wind-swept, sometimes blocked by great snowdrifts. And instead of flocks of a few hundred sheep, shepherds now tended ten to sixteen thousand, and were allotted six horses each. One man remembers how they sheared 10,000 sheep in one day. An Aldbourne boy, born out there, described how, before he was 11 years old, he worked with his father; all the wool, of very fine quality, was sent to England, and he helped to roll great bales down the beach to the special ship that waited there. Another activity was shooting sea-lions for their hides; these were torn into strips to fix collars firmly round the necks of the oxen.

These Wiltshiremen, unaccustomed to anything worse than a fox, now became aware of a far more deady enemy, the puma, also called a Lion or a Catamount. This beast roamed the country at night, and would often kill far more sheep than he needed, sometimes as many as 40, sucking a little blood from each, and returning later to pick up his prey. No wonder the Walronds offered £1 for every dead puma. The shepherds found the best way of killing them was to light a fire at the mouth of one of the caves where they took temporary refuge, and to shoot them as they rushed out panic-stricken. Fortunately now pumas are far scarcer.

Some of these emigrants married and settled down in Patagonia, but several returned to dig themselves back into their native soil, including this Aldbourne boy and his parents. How toughening had been life in Patagonia is illustrated by the way one old man, aged 82, recently fell from top to bottom of his stairs yet, all alone, climbed back to his bed afterwards.

LOCAL GOVERNMENT

The Act of 1888 ushered in an important new era in village-life throughout England. For one thing it abolished the old Court Leet, and the title of Lord of the Manor—not that Aldbourne itself had ever suffered much from the men who bore it, since most of them had been absentees. But even so the landlords and wealthier farmers had previously taken most of the important decisions affecting the welfare of the village. Now at last ordinary men and women were to play a full part.

This new Act, though it introduced only County Councils, was greeted with great enthusiasm in Aldbourne, as 72 lines of verse by a local inhabitant, written at the time of the 1892 election and printed in the *Wiltshire Gazette* testify. These verses also reveal the strength of radicalism in the village, so apparent when Walter Long addressed a meeting in 1884. At this election a Conservative General was

unseated by a Radical named Johnny Fox. I will quote one verse
to illustrate my point:

> *At length the Polling Day arrived,*
> *All beautiful and bright,*
> *Old Pots and Kettles well contrived*
> *To fill us with delight.*

And when the result was known the chief supporters of Fox, referred
to in a refrain as 'Squire Ha-h, and B-s the Baker's Boy', were
triumphantly carried through the village in a cart drawn by a team
of men pretending to be donkeys, then in such common use, who
'pranced about with joy', kicked and whinnied. One of these donkeys
was William Walters, the noted dew-pond maker, whose daughter is
still among us.

The creation of Parish Councils brought even more delights, and
the first election roused intense excitement. The early Minute Books
make fascinating reading.

The Green, always the centre of village life, was the subject of
heated discussion. Should children be allowed to play freely there?
Yes, if the Lord of the Manor, a title that died hard, and the School
Managers, agreed. In 1909 the right of youths to engage in Rounders
and Football was questioned. The fact that Rounders was a dying
game settled that issue, but Football raised a harder problem. Yes,
but with nothing larger than a tennis ball, was the verdict. Should
horses and cattle feed there? No. Should wheeled traffic cross it?
No, the constable must prevent this and notice boards be put up.
But here an old inhabitant protested vehemently. Both these were
ancient rights that had existed ever since the Green had once been
the Village Market Place. A promise to consult an Act of 1910
relating to Village Greens calmed people down. Then someone
suggested that a German gun captured in World War I would be a
pleasant and patriotic gesture; an idea luckily rejected unanimously.

Who should appoint the Town Crier? Who but the Parish
Council? Then there was the Feast. Should boys be allowed to rush
round with water-pistols squirting water down people's necks? No,
but all the same they continued the practice for years. Should the
gipsies set up their roundabouts on the Green? No, but when a
member of the respected Smith family lay dying at Bay House they
might do so to save her from noise; but they and their horses must
always camp in a fenced-in field, and must leave the village by
10 a.m. next morning. Should they come in wartime? Yes, they
brought cheer at a hard time.

The health of the fire-engines, popularly known as Adam and
Eve, caused ceaseless concern, for old age was overtaking them.
After much patching up and many efforts to rejuvenate them, they
were at last, in 1924, put to rest at the back of the church. Then

there were the leather buckets that had helped to extinguish the great fires. Somebody wanted to buy them but the Council refused to sell on any condition whatever. They might, however, be shown at a London exhibition. In 1918 patriotic fervour led to an agreement that all old parish books and records should be sold for waste paper. But years slipped by and fortunately nothing was done about this, till in 1925 the District Auditor refused his consent.

In 1919 Ramsbury asked Aldbourne to back up a request for a railway through the Kennet valley, but the Parish Council let the request lie on the table, and gave a second urgent appeal six months later the same treatment; Ramsbury's concerns were not theirs. Only a line between Swindon and Hungerford interested them.

In September 1929 electric lights shone out for the first time. Hitherto one on the Cross and one on the Engine-house were the only lamps on the Green. Finally the state of the Pond, so dearly loved but so dirty, so overgrown by grass and weeds, so ill-nourished in summer by its natural springs, worried them much. In the year of Queen Elizabeth's Coronation its fate was sealed. A little concrete prison robbed it of its own water supply, and kept it clean and tidy. But never again can Aldbourne claim that it has a real village pond.

Altogether, the more one studies these minutes the greater grows respect for the way year after year public-spirited men, and fortunately women too, now, have tackled the business gallantly, no matter how boring, how controversial, how time-consuming. Deep concern to keep the village alive, healthy and united, has nearly always inspired them; and a sense of humour has often carried them over rough places. The Annual General Meeting is usually a spirited affair.

THE BAND

The Band, started in 1835 by Richard Bunce, has continued for nearly 140 years, and still bears witness to the zeal, musical ability and appreciation of the village. Membership has often gone from father to son. The band began as a brass-and-reed affair, changed to an orchestra, then became the one we know today. The First World War brought the only real break. But even in desolate Flanders, nine of the band cheered themselves and their mates on their own instruments, and four others played in the 19th Divisional Band. In 1925 a queer character, Jimmy White of Foxhill, gave a set of new silver-plated instruments, valued at around £650. Jimmy started life as a bricklayer, became a millionaire through remarkably successful gambling, but at last his luck turned. He lost his whole fortune and took his life: a tragic story redeemed by his great generosity, his lack of snobbery or arrogance.

With these instruments the band has won prizes and success all over Britain, including London, Bristol and Manchester and—more important—it enlivens village life with concerts both in and out of doors.

THE PLAY

Early in the twentieth century a London dramatist of repute, Charles McEvoy, married the miller's daughter from Axford, settled in Aldbourne and helped to make history there. From the very beginning he got on friendly terms with the villagers and delighted in their broad dialect, their simplicity, their directness of speech and their humour. Inspiration came: he would write a village play acted by real village people. Hitherto dramatic activity in the country had come from the houses of the well-to-do and the vicarage; most of them of poor quality and having little true country flavour. McEvoy decided to change all this, and after a little persuasion his village friends agreed to co-operate—among them the postman, the road mender, the baker's wife, the butcher's wife.

In November 1910 he produced his play *The Village Wedding*, a very simple story in which a tramp assaults a bride just after her wedding, and she is rescued after a dramatic fight between tramp and husband. It was acted in the old Malthouse Barn—the one crowned by the maltster weathercock—which became, it is said, the first village theatre in England. London celebrities came to see the play: Granville Barker recited a prologue and Bernard Shaw—who was among the audience—described it as 'very refreshing, very jolly', though he evidently found difficulty in establishing contact with the actors afterwards. One of them said later, 'Yes, well he was a distinguished gentleman but he looked at us as if to say, "I don't want to talk to you. You and I have nothing in common".' This was probably true; Shaw had never met real country people before, and he was completely baffled by their speech.

But the village adored the play. It went down well, too, in Devizes, but when McEvoy rather rashly took it to the Coronet Theatre in London that was a different story. Robbed of its proper setting, spoken in a language that, like Bernard Shaw, the audience for the most part found it hard to understand, while the death of King Edward VII just before its production resulted in a poor attendance and a financial loss, which led to closure of the Malthouse Theatre in 1912.

But the impact of the play both in Wiltshire and in other parts of southern England was great, and the character of village drama slowly but surely changed. And still, after over 60 years, old inhabitants speak of it with pride; the last of the actors died only a year or two ago.

Fifty years later the Green served as background for a far different play, namely 'Dr. Who', and a well-known broadcaster, Johnny Morris, lived for some years in Aldbourne and livened the pub and streets with his unique laughter. Originally he worked as foreman on a farm, and perhaps has never excelled his reproduction in true Wiltshire dialect of the conversation and incidents which he shared.

TWO WORLD WARS

World War I, as in the rest of England, affected the population of Aldbourne far more than the second. One hundred men joined the Forces, many in the Wiltshire Regiment, and 48 lost their lives. But those who safely returned brought with them a knowledge of strange lands and a store of memories; interesting, sad, painful, but also some with a funny side. Such was an experience of the boy who tended the oxen at the Warren in 1911, when he found himself and his comrades sitting, in one of 'the bloodiest bits of country' they had even known; blown on by a hot, dusty wind, no greenness anywhere—then along came their officer and asked, 'Do you know where you are now?' They told him plainly what they thought of it.

'You're in the Garden of Eden!', he replied. 'This cheered them mightily,' said the former ox-boy.

In World War II, though the dead numbered less than a third of those killed in the previous war, it affected the life of the village as a whole more powerfully. Of course there were London children to be cared for, and everyone threw themselves into the salvage business with great energy. Under the directorship of Muriel Foster, bird-lover, naturalist, fisherwoman, over 153 tons of material was collected. Children of all ages took part. The bigger boys scoured the countryside for iron and other metals, bones, paper and rubber, bringing their loads back in boxes fixed on wheels. All was then sorted and stored in sheds and stables, and surprisingly included cannon-balls from the Civil War.

Then came the Americans; the 101st Airborne Division, who, from their camp up at Membury, flew to take part in the Normandy D Day landings. They found good fellowship in Aldbourne, and were, on the whole, popular, even if sometimes they lacked under-standing of the ways of quiet country people. One highly respectable, middle-aged woman was dumbfounded when, after inviting an American to supper as a friendly gesture, she was met by a question with unmistakable intent, 'How much will it cost, please?' At a party to bring village and Americans into closer contact, one old inhabitant drank a small whisky and water with a visitor. 'Have another', said the American, who then, unbeknown to him, filled his glass with neat whisky. The poor man tottered home but fell down as he tried to totter upstairs. It was the first time he had ever been drunk in his life. Another unpopular act was the shooting down of the weathercock on the church tower by an American airman.

But, apart from such incidents, good fellowship prevailed, as a recent visit from the 101st Airborne Veterans' Association testified. Perhaps I may be excused for relating a personal experience. I was staying in New York a few years ago, and came out from a picture gallery to find rain falling in torrents and the world grown horribly dark. So, instead of trying to find a bus I hailed a taxi. When one drew up unwillingly the driver asked where I wanted to go. I named a street on the far west side.

'You'd better take the sub-way', he growled.

'It terrifies me. I'm English.'

'Oh well, get in,' he said, not very graciously.

'Where abouts in England?' he asked as we drove off.

'Wiltshire.'

'Where in Wiltshire?' His voice had grown warmer.

'Aldbourne.'

His manner changed completely. He had been quartered nearby and remembered the good pubs. But he spoke too of the village Green, the tall church tower, the friendly folk. As he set me down outside an ugly block of flats, he muttered,

'You live somewhere better than this.' Yes indeed.

THE CARNIVAL

Like all good villages, Aldbourne celebrates various seasons of the year. At Whitsun, as elsewhere, the old Friendly Societies paraded the village; the Foresters resplendent in green and gold sashes, the Rationals in red and gold; the Hearts of Oak with their acorn and oakleaf, all with silk banners flying, the Band leading them; then a church service, a big dinner in a barn, and sports. At Rogation, walkers of all ages beat the Bounds once more.

In July the age-long Feast unites families and friends, lights up the sky, fills the air, nowadays, with the sad wail of popular music, in place of the old robust tunes from steam organs.

And in September, the Carnival, started in 1925, draws huge crowds for the procession of cars, lorries, individuals on foot and on cycles. Infinite pains are taken, with amazing ingenuity. Though topical and 'trendy' themes are most in evidence, many others draw inspiration from the past; a tinker's car, a gipsy caravan, nursery rhymes, fairy-tales. No matter how cold, how threatening, how wet the weather, all gallantly go through it till the end; the journey to the field under the wooded hill; the long wait while perplexed judges and crowds of spectators wander round, staring, appraising; the slow procession through the village, headed by several Bands and the Carnival Queen and her maidens.

Every year all who merely look on feel fresh admiration for the zest, the gaiety, the stoicism of those who take part; who have dressed up their houses or themselves, or have faced the elements often in the minimum of clothes. When the weather shows no compassion, we say, or think, 'Surely those poor dears will catch their death or cold'. Yet somehow they never do. They are like the old Baptists, who, immersed in an icy pool on a cold day, came to no harm. Throughout the procession the rattle of money-boxes fills the air, and the money goes to various village activities.

SPORT

Football flourishes, but possibly not with its former zest, when some 60 years ago it was played on the downs near Four Barrows.

> 'Ramsbury bull-dogs
> Baydon Squaws
> A'bon Dabchicks beats 'em all',

was a favourite saying.

Up on the old Sugar Way, where long ago robber bands once roamed, sports were held in the second half of the nineteenth century; hurdle races in particular.

Nowadays cricket, sad to say, has declined but tennis is immensely popular.

Weather, Flowers and Birds

WEATHER

I MAKE no apology for including some account of exceptional weather experienced in Aldbourne over more than 100 years, taken from accounts by old inhabitants. Weather always has, and always will be, closely knit with the lives of country people; it affects their work, the cost of their food, and enters continually into their talk. Townsfolk, shut up in offices and shops, seem hardly aware of what is happening outside. Even the weather prophets at Broadcasting House will sometimes tell us to expect 'a fine day, growing warmer', even while snow is falling heavily outside.

Once a Wiltshire farmer, living near Aldbourne, discussed with his foreman whether a field of grass might safely be cut.

'The wireless predicts fine weather. We'd better go ahead', said the farmer. The other shook his head; 'Sarah says as 'twill rain!'

Sarah, a rheumaticky old cow, always stiffened up when rain seemed imminent. But the farmer accepted the B.B.C. report, cut the grass, and watched it drown in a prolonged downpour. 'You see', said the man, 'Sarah was right. We'd best lend her to those London folk. Maybe she'd put some sense into their heads.'

The earliest weather record I have dates from 1799. After a bad summer, 'Harvest began on Sept. 2nd', wrote the farmer, 'and ended only two weeks before Christmas'. That year the price of wheat rose steeply, and a gallon loaf cost 3s. 5½d. These long-drawn-out harvests, due not only to weather but to lack of machines, occur several times. In 1811, a member of the Witts family wrote in his diary; 'About seven in the evening a very terrible thunder and lightning, soon afterwards a cloud-burst, or water-spout with wonderful hail . . . A great body of water entered West St, Calf St, and down Butts and struck in a body against Mr Wells' Bell shop . . . it entered the Malthouse and covered the malt on the lower floors; the cottages below were filled with water and muck. The sight very awful and never anything like it seen by the inhabitants.'

In August, 1863, as some labourers, gathering in a field of Sainfoin, lifted the last load the pleasant breeze turned into a terrific whirlwind. The men, crouching under the rick, saw the wagon (from which the horse had been unharnessed) carried away for a considerable distance; had the wheels not locked themselves it would have gone still further. 1868 brought an excessively hot, dry summer, and the death of several people, supposedly from sunstroke. And this in spite of the fact that their own straw-plait hats protected their heads. Two years later it was again lamentably dry, rain from April till October was infinitesimal. An unusually hard winter followed, with heavy snowfalls. The nights of 13 and 14 November were beautified by a wonderful display of shooting stars, known afterwards as the great 'Star Shower'.

'A never-to-be-forgotten sight', wrote one chronicler; 'they were like a lot of arrows all pointing the same way.'

In 1878–9 there came still more severe weather, with bedroom jugs constantly frozen, then a long, rainy spell. 'It was always wet on Sundays, week after week,' says the reporter sadly. In 1881 again a bitter winter; deep snow, followed by continuous rain.

In 1888 extremely cold weather succeeded a wet summer. Harvest only started at the end of September, and some corn still lay in the November fields. The same thing happened again three years later. High winds and torrents of rain made harvesting impossible for days at a time. At Woodsend fields remained uncut at Christmas. The problems that beset all farmers were doubly difficult in those days. 19 April 1908, saw the beginning of a series of blizzards unparalleled for that time of year, and which raged through Easter week. Round Aldbourne snow lay over a foot deep, with drifts up Stock Lane and on Baydon Hill of five to six ft. Two Poor-Law officers returning from Marlborough through Aldbourne tramped beside their pony-trap with its wheels almost buried in snow. On Salisbury Plain a man, out walking after the worst of the storm, saw an arm waving from a drift. He came just in time to save a sergeant carrying despatches and nearly dead with exhaustion; farmers everywhere were busy digging out sheep.

With the summer of 1921 came a terrible drought. All ponds and wells except one ran dry. From the only well that held a little water, beyond the doorway in the wall opposite the Forge, a few people were privileged to fill their buckets, but the main supply was brought from the Kennet in milk-cans. When a fire broke out in West Street, 100 gallons were fetched in that way.

Late in December 1939 and in January 1940 Aldbourne shared with the rest of England a continuous frost, culminating in rain that froze as it fell. Every leaf, every blade of grass, was encased in ice. Pigeons were frozen on the trees; sheep turned into cascades of tingling icicles. Then a sudden thaw set in, followed by heavy rain, and on 3 February 1940 the village woke to hear torrents of water streaming along the streets. Ivy Cottage was an island; the Pond lost in the surrounding water, only the top of its railings visible.

A pig was washed from its sty and drowned, as were many hens. In Castle Street the water raced down from the hill, and someone reported that it ran through her cottage like a Highland stream. In Lottage people took to their bedrooms while their furniture floated about below. Not till the evening did the flood begin to abate, and by that time all gumboots had been sold out.

Though lesser floods had occurred from time to time never, within human memory, was there one to equal this. But no lives were lost, and since nearly everybody enjoys spectacular weather in retrospect, so did Aldbourne people continue to find 'The Great Flood' an exhilarating topic of conversation for a long while.

FLOWERS AND BIRDS

Before ending this survey I want to say a little bit about something knit closely to the heart of any village, its flowers and birds. Aldbourne cannot boast such a variety of flowers as places with a river and water meadows. I have checked 211 species, but an expert botanist would find more. Of these the dandelion might be named its patron saint, glowing on every verge and bank, sending its beautiful, mischievous flakes into every garden. No wonder it survived the Ice Age. It may be that the widespread making of dandelion wine in the past kept its number down a bit. An old woman coming in with a pail was a welcome sight.

Two other plants, abundant but more desirable, are cow parsley, foaming along Whitsun waysides, and the big wild geranium, turning the verges of upland roads into blue rivers. A sky-blue variety grows in one little lonely lane, and a white one elsewhere. An uncommon plant, hiding in a remote copse, is herb paris, its green flowers encircled by four big leaves and bearing a black berry; it was once used as a cure for madness. Other copses are rich in Solomon's seal and woodruff, which some housewives laid among their linen. In at least one wood grows that pale parasite, toothwort; not much to look at you may say, but wait till you see its semi-transparent petals turn rosy in the sunset.

Downland flowers have been sadly depleted by intensive ploughing, but still get a chance to survive in some places. Eye-bright, widely used once for a lotion to make old eyes young again, with its dark purple eye set in a fringed white face, is one of the most endearing. In Devon, children were warned never to pick a piece because, they were told, a robin might peck out their own eyes. A secretive little plant on Peaks Down is the frog orchis. The bee orchis has grown sadly scarce, perhaps from ruthless picking. The new M4 motorway, cutting through a stretch of our downs, destroyed one especially good patch of pyramids. Sometimes you may meet a bit of sainfoin on downland verges, reminder of a time when rosy-pink fields added much to the Wiltshire landscape.

A shrub that possibly no other Wiltshire village possesses is the dogwood, *Cornus mas*, or Cornelian cherry; not a true native—it comes from Austria—but we accept it gladly. In February, for some 50 years a long hedge of it has burst into yellow bloom when all others are still in sombre black. But it never lives up to its second title, Cornelian cherry; no berry ever appears on it. Perhaps because of its colour yellow hammers love that upland hedge. Another yellow flower that is happy on our upland banks is the yellow toadflax.

On the Sugar Way grows, or grew a short while ago, a clump of white helleborine, and up till a few years ago the nettle-leaved bellflower (*C. trachelium*) grew there too, and also in a ditch near the Shepherd's Rest.

Cobbett, after riding a little farther north on his way to High-worth, wrote, 'I saw at a village called Stratton ... the finest campanula I ever saw in my life ... the main stem was more than 4ft high'. Since he was a little given to exaggeration this may well have been the same bellflower which used to be so plentiful, though it might have been the giant campanula (*C. Latifolia*).

BIRDS

The swift has the best claim to be our signature bird. From early May till mid-August he and his fellows sweep wildly, excitedly round the village and nest where given the chance. But the collared dove, that rather unwelcome newcomer, is the one who makes his presence most conspicuous throughout the year with his frustrated, monotonous call, so much less melodious than that of the woodpigeon.

As bird-tables and baskets testify, tits abound; great and blue tits especially, with an occasional marsh or coal tit. The beautiful long-tailed tits, with voices like tiny silver bells, though often seen in our trees and hedges, seldom come to nut baskets, though hard weather sometimes brings a nuthatch. A few lucky people get visits from that handsome fellow, the great spotted woodpecker, and, all too rarely nowadays, the green woodpecker. Numerous greenfinches vie with tits for nuts.

A kestrel is fond of circling the church tower, and hobbies occur on Peaks and round North Farm. A few sparrow hawks appear on the edges of the village, and now and then a buzzard soars over the Southward or Upper Upham; while a peregrine has stayed a night once or twice on Peaks. Owls are often heard at twilight or by night, both the tawny and the barn owl, but, sad to say, the latter is becoming rare. A few years ago one nested regularly in Cor's barn, and then in a tall elm tree close by till a cruel wind felled it: the hollow trunk was stuffed with his pellets. An exciting winter visitor is the short-eared owl. No less than seven were sweeping early this year over Peaks, often quite low, but keeping watchful guard from their great yellow eyes. One took up residence in a turnip-field close to a crop of buckwheat, where enormous flocks of small birds assembled. Undoubtedly some must have disappeared down his throat. Yellow hammers are far less common nowadays, but they love the long hedge of *Cornus mas* on top of Greenhill, where they look strikingly beautiful among the bright yellow blossoms.

Rare visitors include a ring ouzel, on his way to higher country, and some four years ago a nutcracker from Northern Eurpoe, with his formidable beak and raucous cry. Early in the century a hurdle-maker up in the woods still remembers hearing and seeing this strange bird. On warm summer evenings of most years quails, those clever ventriloquists, utter their low, unmistakable flow of high-pitched notes in cornfields round the village. Goldfinches nest in some gardens, particularly in one wild, deserted one. Because we have so much thatch, wrens breed freely, and some of us have the pleasure of watching nine or ten slipping out of their nest for the first time. Pied wagtails trip about and, all too seldom, someone catches the flash of a yellow one.

Because no real river runs through the village water-birds are scarce. However, a year or two ago when our winterbourne reached an unusual depth, a dipper skimmed along it for a few days, and a kingfisher has paid a fleeting visit to a garden pool. Though swans are seldom found here the rhythmic beat of their wings is not infrequently heard as they pass between Coate Water and the Kennet.

The dabchick is hardly likely to be seen again on our diminutive, sophisticated pond, but he pushes his way up the bourne when it runs freely as far as Hodder's Bridge, and so do redshanks.

ELEVEN

Goodbye to the Village

AFTER wandering round, reading and talking about the village for many years nostalgia inevitably winds its insidious web about you. You dream of newly-cast bells setting off on their long journeys over the downs; of deft fingers weaving the beautiful 'brilliants' straw plait; of a girl trying on her bridal home-made willow hat. Or you seem to hear the axe, hammer, plane, busy making those handsome chairs, as good today as they were 50 years ago.

Again, you may look resentfully at the stream of cars passing through at a ridiculous and illegal pace, and sigh for the sound of horses' feet and of the bells round their necks; the slow unobtrusive rumble of wheels. And you wish that children could still safely roll their hoops and boys kick their football about the streets as they did early in the century. Potted music pouring through open doors and windows make you long for men whistling on their way to work, and people singing their own songs, playing their own pipes, fiddles or accordions.

But how useless all that is. Instead, it may be as well to remember that a man and woman were flogged in the Market Place for taking wood from the Chase; that starving labourers gnawed raw turnips to appease their hunger, broke up machines and set fire to ricks; that people made muck-heaps on the Green, or sat, cold and miserable in the stocks; that children left school at ten and worked 12 hours a day. And you may also reflect that some of those playing round the Market Cross today may one day be telling their own children how peaceful a place the village was 60 years ago; of how many young, middle-aged, old, 'beat' the 18 miles of the parish bounds on foot; of boys rushing about on push-bikes; of the Carnival that brought colour and gaiety as summer ended.

For even those things might die. You can never tell what lies ahead. But at least we can accept the present gratefully, if with certain reservations. This village of some 1,550 souls is growing; sad in many ways but inevitable. People must be housed, and who can blame those who, working in a noisy town, long for the peace of the countryside when their day is over? Meanwhile, though

Aldbourne welcomes newcomers who add to, and share its life, it looks more coolly at people who use it merely as a place to sleep in, to exercise their dogs at weekends, and to give noisy parties.

I have tried, and I know only too well that I have only half succeeded, to present the image of a village with a heart that still beats soundly. A walk round it in afternoon or evening testifies to that. Babies are everywhere; children dash out of school in the highest of spirits, always ready with smiles and hullos; old men sun themselves in front of the pond as they have year after year. As evening comes they can move if they so will to a seat on the other side of the pond.

At least 14 different societies testify to the variety of interests that enrich village life. Every winter a band of actors presents a pantomime with liveliness and ingenuity, in spite of the fact that most of them do a hard day's work before they rehearse or perform. A strong branch of the Civic Society exists. The Women's Institute, though it has, like most others, its feebler moments, at its best certainly stimulates the minds and imaginations of its members, and always fosters good human relationships. The Band continues to liven, refresh, and to gain fresh honours, while recorder-playing children make their own music. And in one important respect at least Aldbourne's heart is sounder than in those old days when religious dissension was rife, when dissenting preachers risked loss of liberty and heavy fines; when an almost tangible barrier stood between churchgoers and those who wished to worship in a different way. Now Anglicans and Dissenters meet regularly in each other's building and share each other's activities. There would be no need today for old William Wild to preach out-of-doors, and people be forced to climb to Baydon to hear him. He would be welcomed at St Michael's.

Of course, as with all true villages and most families there are occasional skirmishes, occasional flare-ups, but these usually die down quickly.

And with that we leave Aldbourne, set among 'the wild, wide, houseless downs' of a Wiltshire parson's song when he welcomed a queen to his village a few miles away. These downs, from one point of view, have suffered much from the plough, but some remain unspoilt, to walk on, to look at, to nourish large flocks of sheep. Green, fawn, grey, or white with snow, swept by cloud shadows, they vary continually.

And above all the bells still peal out from the church tower, as they have done now for nearly 400 years.

Reference Sources

Abbreviations used
V.C.H.—Victoria County History (Wiltshire); D.N.B.—Dictionary of National Biography; Enc. Brit.—*Encyclopaedia Britannica*; W.N.C. —*Wiltshire News* Cuttings (Devizes Museum); Q.S.G.R.—Quarter Session Great Rolls; D of L—Duchy of Lancaster.

In and Around the Village
James Penny (Aldbourne Cross); Minutes of Parish Council; Enclosure Act of 1805; R. P. de B. Nicholson, C.Eng., M.I.Mech.E.; Information in Inkpen Papers from the Great Rolls; The Black Prince's Register, Pt. IV; Computus Roll of the Reeve; O.L. Depositions for 1551; The Great Rolls; Survey of D of L woods in S. England; D of L Records; Letters of Henry VIII; D of L: Report of Overseers and Depositions for 1551; Abstracts of Wilts., ed. E. A. Fry; Thomas Davis: *Agriculture in the County of Wilts.*; Calendar of I.P.M. (Public Records Office) Vol. IV; John Aubrey: *Natural History of Wiltshire*; Prof. R. Bradley: *Aldbourne Chase and Warren* (1729); R. Walrond: *History of the Walronds*; Q.S.G.R. for 17th Century, ed. B. Cunnington; Rushworth Collections, III, 7a.

War, Peace and Dissent
Diary of Sgt Henry Foot (in the collection of Tracts covering the Civil War in the Brit. Mus.); Clarendon: *History of the Great Rebellion*; A. R. Stedman: *Marlborough and the Kennet Valley*; V.C.H. Vol. III; Archdeaconal Records, Sarum Diocesan Registry.

Village Industries
H. B. Walters: *The Church Bells of Wiltshire*; W. C. Lukis: *Church Bells*; V.C.H. Vol. IV; Information received from M. V. Norris, Guildford; Records of Mears & Steinbank, Bell Founders; Churchwardens' Accounts; Court Leet Records; L. Wheeler: *Chertsey Abbey*; Will of Edward Witts, 1688; Census for 1851; R. Pocock: *Travels through England*, vol. 1 (Camden Society); Bishop Mant: *History of the Church of Ireland*, vol. II; The Bishop's Register; Enc.

Brit.; E. Nesbit: *Grammar of Textile Design*; Information received from the city archivist, The Hague; A. R. Stedman: *Marlborough and Upper Kennet Country*; information received from Dr J. de L. Mann; J. C. Dory: *History of the Straw Plait Industry*; Daniel Defoe: *Tour throughout the Whole Island of Great Britain*; Vol. V of Pamphlets of the Society for the Betterment of the Poor; W.N.C.; for information on the Willow Trade. Article by Alfred Williams referred to in the text. An article in an early number of the *Star* recorded in Major Inkpen's collection, but unfortunately not dated: Inkpen himself, in 1930, recorded conversations with men who had been concerned with the willow trade; Richard Steward in D.N.B.

Hard Times and the Enclosure Act
W.N.C. (W. Chandler); *Salisbury Journal*, January 1832; B. & J. L. Hammond: *The Village Labourer*; Trade Directory, 1792; Arthur Young: *Annals of Agriculture*; Quarter Sessions Records for Wiltshire; W. H. Hudson: *A Shepherd's Life*; Enclosure Act, 1805; D.N.B.

The Village in Later Days
Information on Patagonia received from W. Woolford and H. Fisher; *Account of all Schools of the Labouring Classes in the County of Wilts.*, 7 February 1859.

Weather, Flowers and Birds
W.N.C. vol. XI; Report by Mary Gillingham, 1930; D. Grose: *Flora of Wiltshire* (for E. Sophia Todd).

Index

Also from Alan Sutton Publishing by the same author

An Idler on the Shropshire Borders

August 1930 found Ida Gandy and her two small sons setting off to explore Shropshire in an ancient Baby Austin. Here, by chance, she found the country practice her doctor husband had dreamed of and which was to become their home for fifteen extremely happy years.

From detailed diaries she writes with deep affection of their life in the village of Clunbury and the beautiful surrounding countryside; of walking the hills either alone or with her children; of the trout stream at the foot of the garden; of boating there or across fields flooded to form one vast lake; of border castles; of Clun sheep; of village broadcasts and of birds – curlew, heron, raven and kite.

Shropshire people today and country lovers everywhere will enjoy this delightful view of a county which encompasses both the picturesque and the scenic.

Round About the Little Steeple

Unavailable for some time, but now reprinted in a new edition, *Round About the Little Steeple* is an account of Ida Gandy's downland Wiltshire village, Bishops Cannings, as it was in the early seventeenth century. In particular, she tells of George Ferebe, the parson of St Mary's Church, 'an ingenious man and an excellent musician', who enriches his church with a peal of bells and an organ, preaches eloquently and trains the young people in music. When Queen Anne, wife of James I, passes by on her way from Bath, members of the church choir sing to her a song of Ferebe's own composing; later, the King himself is entertained with a football match.

Using the Church Registers, Court Books, old deeds and tithe maps, and her intimate knowledge of the village, Ida Gandy describes the parish and its inhabitants in Ferebe's day: John Ernle, Lord of the Manor; the prolific Slops and Ruddles; a village Dick Whittington; and the persecuted Withers. Everyone interested in local history, especially those living in and around the Pewsey Vale, will find this book makes fascinating reading.

Staying with the Aunts

Every summer Ida Gandy and her sisters used to visit the Aunts – her five spinster aunts who lived together at Eling Manor on the edge of the New Forest:

Aunt Selina – a buttoned-up little figure, hiding away in her small room at the end of the passage
Aunt Margaret – spending long dreamy hours in her studio and growing ever more eccentric
Aunt Carry – broad-hipped and capable, and managing everything with infinite wisdom
Aunt Louisa – alive with insatiable curiosity
Aunt Mary – arch and slightly kittenish, but possessing a deep social conscience

The 'World of the Aunts', they thought, must *always* have been like that. Then, when the last aunt died, Ida discovered their letters and read of their youth in the Wiltshire village of Baverstock and in Salisbury, where their father was Archdeacon; of what had caused them to become the people she knew; and of their visits to their *own* aunts and what they thought about them. . . .

A Wiltshire Childhood

Ida Gandy spent her early childhood in a remote and secluded village, cut off from the rest of the world by the downs. The gabled red-bricked vicarage where she lived – often the centre of village activity – was a warm, friendly and rambling house.

But for Ida, 'real life' took place out-of-doors, and this charming book is a delightful record of remembered pleasures and adventures, family picnics and childish explorations, of long summer days and wild winter expeditions, of jumping the ha-ha and learning to ride, of bees and pineapple pippins, and rhubarb wine at haymaking.

Seen with the magical freshness of a child growing up, Ida's account vividly describes times and people long dead with an incisive precision. *A Wiltshire Childhood* is an unforgettable and intimate portrait of a country childhood, which cannot fail to charm the reader.